THE GREAT
AMERICAN
RECIPE
COOKBOOK

REGIONAL CUISINE AND FAMILY FAVORITES FROM THE HIT TV SHOW

100 Recipes from the Contestants, Tiffany Derry, Leah Cohen, Graham Elliot, and Alejandra Ramos

BenBella Books, Inc.
Dallas, TX

BenBella

BenBella Books, Inc.
10440 N. Central Expressway
Suite 800
Dallas, TX 75231
benbellabooks.com
Send feedback to feedback@benbellabooks.com.

BenBella is a federally registered trademark.

Printed in the United States of America
10 9 8 7 6 5 4 3 2 1

Library of Congress Control Number: 2022935034
ISBN 9781637740156 (paper over board)
ISBN 9781637740217 (electronic)

Editing by Claire Schulz
Copyediting by Karen Wise
Proofreading by Sarah Vostok and Lisa Story
Indexing by WordCo Indexing Services, Inc.
Text design and composition by Faceout Studio, Paul Nielsen
Cover design by Sarah Avinger
Cover photography by Fred + Elliott Photography
Printed by Versa Press

**Special discounts for bulk sales are available.
Please contact bulkorders@benbellabooks.com.**

CONTENTS

INTRODUCTION

Welcome to *The Great American Recipe Cookbook*! Here you'll find more than one hundred recipes that celebrate the incredible diversity and big flavors of American cuisine. When you think of American food, maybe you think of a Fourth of July picnic or the familiar dishes that bring your family to the table every week. Perhaps it's a regional icon like New England clam chowder or Carolina barbecue. Or it could be a dish that represents a fusion of international flavors with a local spin. American food is all of that and more. These recipes represent the dynamic story of America . . . told through the foods we love.

Recipes, like stories, say so much about the time, place, and person from which they come. Our favorite dishes are the common threads that connect us all, providing tangible links to our identities, our memories and our experiences, as well as to each other. When we share the recipe for a home-cooked meal—whether we're divulging our secret for the perfect chicken adobo or talking through the steps to a three-generations-old Sunday gravy—we are also sharing pieces of our heritage and culture. That spirit of sharing is what *The Great American Recipe* is all about. Well, that, and some truly delicious food!

On the first season of *The Great American Recipe*, ten home cooks competed over eight weeks to see whose dishes were worthy of the title "Great American Recipe." These home cooks represent culinary cultural legacies from around the world and around

the country, from the Pacific Northwest to Puerto Rico. In these pages, we've collected their best recipes from the show (as well as a few dishes from the host and judges!). Welcome us into your kitchen to experience the foods that have meant the most to them and their families—and discover new favorites your own family will love.

The show, and these recipes, would not be complete without the expert guidance and culinary knowledge of our host and judges. As a lifestyle and food contributor and writer, host Alejandra Ramos has created hundreds of recipes that combine the Puerto Rican foods she grew up eating in New York City with the dishes and flavors she's fallen in love with along the way. Tiffany Derry is an award-winning chef whose acclaimed restaurants in Texas celebrate the soul of Southern farm-to-table cooking. Leah Cohen is a celebrated chef, restaurateur, and cookbook author whose cuisine combines classical Western cooking with the robust flavors of her Filipina heritage. Growing up on naval bases around the world, Graham Elliot was exposed to cuisine from every continent. His culinary gift earned his eponymous Chicago restaurant a rare two Michelin stars, and he eventually returned to the Hawaii of his youth, blending the local flavors of the islands in to his inventive cuisine. Look for delectable recipes from Alejandra, Tiffany, Leah, and Graham throughout this book, as well.

Ingredients of *The Great American Recipe Cookbook*

Here's what you'll find in these pages.

Appetizers, Snacks, and Sides

Look here for a collection of delicious bites to serve before or alongside a meal (or in between!).

Soups, Stews, and Salads

Here's where you'll find a range of dishes that are perfect to start a meal and hearty enough to serve as a main course. (And if you're feeling ambitious, some recipes also include instructions for the delicious homemade breads the cooks like to serve alongside!)

Handhelds

This chapter is all about dishes that satisfy, with no silverware required—we're talking sandwiches, tacos, and pizza.

Family Dinners

These are quintessential meals to bring everybody to the table. You'll find a range of recipes, from classic meat-and-veggie combos to rice and pasta dishes. Many of these are the weeknight-friendly favorites our home cooks turn to again and again.

Holidays and Special Occasions

Turn to this chapter when you need a meal to impress on a special occasion or a dish worthy of a holiday feast.

Brunch

These recipes start your day on a delicious note—egg dishes, biscuits, and a sweet pumpkin bread.

Desserts and Pastry

No meal is complete without a little something sweet. Here you'll find a variety of treats, like cakes, cookies, pudding, and pie.

MEET THE COOKS

Irma Cadiz

Irma's cooking is rooted in the Dominican and Puerto Rican food she grew up eating, and preparing her mother's recipes is her tribute to her family's heritage. Irma's signature dish, Mofongo con Camarones (page 20), is a popular Caribbean comfort

food made from mashed plantains and shrimp. Raised in a multicultural environment in Rochester, New York, Irma experienced a wide range of cuisines; she now resides in New York City and

loves taking part in the city's richly diverse culinary scene. Taking what she has learned along the way, Irma puts creative spins on her personal recipes when she cooks for her adult children and extended family.

Bambi Daniels

Bambi describes her cooking as Southern soul food because everything that she cooks has a hint of

her South Carolina roots and the classic comfort foods she was raised on. Bambi grew up on her family's farm, where they prepared all their meals using only what they grew and everyone had a role in the kitchen, from snapping peas to chopping

greens. As a mother, she loves preparing home-cooked meals for her children and their friends

because she believes walls are broken down when people sit down to eat, and when they sit down at her dinner table, they instantly become family. Bambi bases her signature dish, Southern Smoke Mac and Cheese (page 28), on a recipe that's been passed down from generation to generation and is still a family favorite in her house.

Robin Daumit

Living in the Chesapeake Bay area, Robin loves to cook with fresh seafood, especially blue crab and oysters, which are staples in her dishes. She has a passion for fresh ingredients from her own garden, including figs, peppers, and fresh herbs. In fact, she has had a fig tree in the garden of every home she has owned; the tree represents prosperity, health, and well-being in all areas of life, and was the inspiration for her signature dish: Fish in a Fig Leaf (page 145). As a single parent of four and now a grandmother, Robin loves whipping up recipes

she has collected throughout her lifetime to share with her family—her style is a true melting pot of Mediterranean and Middle Eastern cuisine from her mother's Syrian heritage and the regional foods of her home state of Maryland. She has made it her life's purpose to pass on the traditions of her family's favorite Middle Eastern dishes.

Brian Leigh

Originally from Ohio, Brian now calls Kentucky home, where he cooks hearty, homestyle meals for his wife and family. Brian prides himself on his rustic Southern cooking infused with the flavors of his Hungarian and German heritage. His bold dishes are big on funky, fer-

mented ingredients like sauerkraut, which his family used in many of their Eastern European–inspired dishes. His mother and father are his biggest influences in the kitchen, and he loves to create their

most treasured family recipes. Brian credits his father for his passion for barbecuing, which led to him starting his own award-winning Barbecue Sauce and

Rub company. His love of barbecued meats and smoky, funky flavors are combined in Brian's signature dish: Cast Iron Ribeye with Blue Cheese and Balsamic Steak Sauce, served alongside Barbecue Brussels Sprouts (page 156).

Silvia Martinez

Silvia's cooking style centers on traditional Mexican and Californian fresh ingredients. Silvia grew up in

Guanajuato in central Mexico, preparing authentic dishes that she learned as a child from her grandmother and mother. Those family recipes are her biggest inspiration. After Silvia met her husband, they moved to California's central coast region, where they are currently raising their two sons. Silvia loves to meld her family's favorite recipes with American classics to connect with other Latina parents—

for whom she is deeply committed to fostering a dynamic community. She has created a blog to share her personal recipes that became a huge hit. Silvia's signature dish is Red Chilaquiles with red roasted salsa and sunny-side-up egg

(page 193), a popular Mexican breakfast dish she makes with extra crispy tortilla chips.

Christina McAlvey

Christina calls her food "Fili-fusion": a mash-up of Filipino flavors and her favorite world cuisines. She loves to create healthier versions of her family's favorite Filipino recipes, like the Chicken Adobo she learned to make from her dad as a child. Her signature dish, Chicken Adobo Bowls (page 101), is a leaner version that swaps in chicken breast instead of thighs, alongside fragrant garlic brown rice and a hearty kale salad. Born and raised in the Midwest, Christina appreciates both traditional American classics and the recipes she has collected along the way. Christina and her husband now call Portland, Oregon, home. She enjoys an active and healthy lifestyle including cooking dishes featuring locally sourced, organic, and gluten-free ingredients.

Foo Nguyen

Foo's Vietnamese heritage is his greatest culinary influence, and he loves to prepare the beloved recipes that he was raised on. When Foo was two years old, his family immigrated to Cincinnati, Ohio, where he learned to combine East Asian flavors with Midwestern comfort food classics. Each year at Christmastime, his mother gave out egg rolls stuffed with pork, shrimp, and crab to their family and com-

munity. Foo keeps that family tradition alive in his signature dish, Mom's Gifted Egg Rolls (page 11). He and his Korean American wife now live in Orange County, California, and he loves to cook various East Asian–style dishes for their two daughters.

Dan Rinaldi

Raised among a multigenerational Italian family, Dan learned to cook treasured favorite recipes in his grandmother's kitchen. Sunday dinners were a staple of his childhood—and it wasn't uncommon for this Rhode Island family to bring their pasta to the beach on a Sunday afternoon and share a meal outdoors. Dan is influenced by his Italian heritage and the fresh regional seafood from his home near Providence, and he takes pride

in carrying on his family recipes and highlighting the rich Italian community that he is a part of in Rhode Island. Dan has a thirty-two-year career as a firefighter and takes immense joy in cooking hearty Italian meals for his colleagues, like his Sunday Gravy with meatballs (page 122). Based on his grandmother's meat sauce recipe, it's a firehouse favorite that's equally loved by his grandchildren.

Tony Scherber

Born in South Korea, Tony was adopted as an infant and raised in Minneapolis, Minnesota. Tony's adoptive mother would cook his family dishes from an old Korean cookbook so that he could stay connected to his culture. In high school, Tony aspired to be a chef and would help his mom in the kitchen whenever he could. Now, he works as a Sport

Operation Specialist; in his free time, he loves to impress his friends and family with home-cooked meals or take them to discover a new restaurant. Tony's cooking combines his family's Midwestern roots and his Korean heritage. His signature dish, Korean Chicken Tacos (page 86), are sweet, spicy, and full of flavor—representing the fusion of his cultures and his love of big, bold flavors.

Nikki Tomaino-Allemand

When they immigrated to the United States, Nikki's family brought with them their recipe for Italian Baccala (page 178)—a salted cod stew that traditionally kicks off the Feast of the Seven Fishes in Italy. Learning to make it became a rite of passage among her family, and the traditional Italian dish is now her signature—though Nikki's cooking also combines her Seattle upbringing and her passion for travel, which has expanded her repertoire to include East Asian cuisine (now a favorite). Her table is full of fresh seafood and her home-grown herbs and vegetables. She now lives in Idaho with her husband and two sons where she started her own meal delivery service for other busy moms.

Appetizers, Snacks, and Sides

Choriqueso 3

Barley and Lamb Stuffed Grape Leaves 5

Vietnamese Spring Rolls 8

Mom's Gifted Egg Rolls 11

Mandu 13
(Pot Stickers)

Lola's Lumpia Shanghai 16

Spicy Fried Chicken Drumettes 18

Mofongo con Camarones 20
(Fried Mashed Plantains with Shrimp)

Rhode Island–Style Fried Calamari 23

Bacalaitos 24
(Fish Fritters)

Spinach-Stuffed Squid over Rainbow Chard 26

Southern Smoke Mac and Cheese 28

Baked Stuffed Quahogs 30

Linguiça Beans 31

Kimchi Fried Rice 33

Fried Zucchini Flowers 34

Choriqueso

with Homemade Flour Tortillas

Silvia

A big hit with the kids, choriqueso is a popular Mexican snack made with spicy chorizo and melted cheese and served with flour or corn tortillas and salsa or guacamole. Fresh-made flour tortillas are irresistible, and this recipe explains how to make them at home. It's easier than you think, and they go amazingly well with choriqueso. **Serves 6**

Flour tortillas

2 cups all-purpose flour, plus more for dusting

5 tablespoons lard

1 teaspoon salt

¾ cup boiling water

Chopped guacamole

2 large avocados, peeled, pitted, and chopped

1 Roma tomato, chopped

¼ white onion, chopped

1–2 serrano peppers, chopped

Chopped fresh cilantro to taste

Juice of 1 lime

Salt to taste

Choriqueso

1–2 teaspoons olive oil

10 ounces pork chorizo

1 pound shredded Mexican cheese blend, Oaxaca cheese, or queso quesadilla

1. In a mixer, using the dough hook, knead together the flour, lard, salt, and boiling water until the dough is smooth and warm. Divide the dough into 12 balls, cover with a kitchen towel, and let them rest for 20 minutes.

2. Meanwhile, combine all the chopped guacamole ingredients in a large bowl and toss gently to mix. Cover and refrigerate until ready to serve.

3. Warm up a cast iron skillet or comal over medium-high heat.

4. Spread a little flour on a work surface. Using a rolling pin, roll one of the dough balls into a circle 4–5 inches in diameter. Place the tortilla in the hot skillet or comal. When the dough has changed color from beige to off-white and started forming bubbles, about 15 seconds, turn it over. Cook for another 13–15 seconds and turn it over again. The tortilla should have golden-brown spots where the bubbles formed. If it takes more than 15 seconds per side to cook, increase the temperature a little bit. Place the tortilla in a clean kitchen towel to keep it warm. Repeat to make all the tortillas.

5. Preheat the oven to 400 degrees F.

(recipe continues)

6. Heat the oil in a large skillet over medium-high heat. Add the chorizo and cook, breaking up the meat, until crispy, 8–10 minutes.

7. Put 2 tablespoons of chorizo into each of six ramekins. Fill the ramekins with cheese, then mix the chorizo and cheese for a few seconds. The cheese will melt slightly and create more space in the ramekins. Fill up the ramekins with the rest of the cheese.

8. Place the ramekins on a rimmed baking sheet and bake for 4–5 minutes, or until the cheese is completely melted.

9. Serve immediately with the flour tortillas and chopped guacamole on the side.

Barley and Lamb Stuffed Grape Leaves

Robin

Yes, I was that weird mom who packed stuffed grape leaves in my children's lunches when I sent them off to school! Those stuffed grape leaves were probably more enticing to their teachers than their peers, but I knew my kids were well fed while away from home. Stuffed grape leaves are as diversely prepared as the multiple Mediterranean cooks who make them. These barley and lamb stuffed grape leaves, served with a labneh dip with toasted pine nuts and sun-dried tomatoes, are a somewhat simplified recipe for busy American cooks, without the laborious steps traditionally used to make them. **Makes 40 grape leaves**

Stuffed grape leaves

1 tablespoon unsalted butter

1 garlic clove, minced

1 teaspoon fine sea salt, divided

½ cup pearled barley, rinsed

2 cups boiling water

2 tablespoons olive oil, plus more for brushing

1 large shallot, finely chopped

1 pound ground lamb

¼ cup fresh oregano leaves, plus a few sprigs for garnish

2 lemons, 1 zested and juiced, 1 thinly sliced

2 tablespoons grated Pecorino Romano cheese

40 large, tender grape leaves, stemmed and rinsed (see note)

Coarse sea salt, for sprinkling

Dipping sauce

1½ cups plain full-fat yogurt

¼ cup pine nuts, toasted

¼ cup sun-dried tomatoes, chopped

Olive oil, for drizzling

2 tablespoons fresh oregano leaves

---

1. Melt the butter in a saucepan over medium heat. Add the garlic and ½ teaspoon of the salt and sauté briefly, just until fragrant. Add the barley and cook, stirring, until the barley is toasted and just starts to stick. Add the boiling water. Cover the pan, lower the heat, and simmer until tender, about 25 minutes. Drain.

2. Heat the olive oil in a large skillet over medium heat. Add the shallot and cook until softened, about 1 minute. Add the ground lamb, oregano, and remaining ½ teaspoon salt and cook, breaking apart the meat, until cooked through, about 10 minutes. Add the lemon juice and grated cheese and stir. Add the cooked barley and stir well.

3. Preheat the oven to 325 degrees F. Line a large baking pan with parchment paper.

4. Lay out the grape leaves on a sheet of parchment paper and cover with another sheet of parchment paper. Taking one grape leaf at a time, place about 1 tablespoon of the filling in the center, fold the

(recipe continues)

sides over, and roll it up cigar style. Place the roll in the lined baking pan, brush lightly with a little olive oil, and add a pinch of coarse salt and a little lemon zest (reserve some zest for the dipping sauce).

5. When all the rolls are finished, loosely cover the pan with aluminum foil and bake for about 10 minutes, just long enough to warm and crisp the leaves. Meanwhile, put the yogurt in a small bowl. Sprinkle the pine nuts and sun-dried tomatoes across the top of the yogurt, drizzle with a bit of olive oil, and sprinkle the oregano leaves and remaining lemon zest on top.

6. Transfer the stuffed grape leaves to a serving platter and garnish with lemon slices and oregano. Serve with the yogurt dipping sauce.

Note: If your grape leaves are small, you will need 80 leaves, to layer 2 leaves per roll.

Vietnamese Spring Rolls

Foo

with Spicy Hoisin Peanut Dipping Sauce

These spring rolls (also known as summer rolls) are light and versatile portable foods that make for a healthy snack. The contrasting flavors and textures marry perfectly: the savory pork and shrimp pair well with the cool fresh cucumber and herbs, while the fluffy and soft vermicelli noodles nicely offset the crunchy fried egg roll wrapper. The spicy hoisin peanut dipping sauce is a perfect accompaniment to the rolls. **Serves 6**

Spring rolls

1 knob ginger

1 stalk lemongrass

1 pound pork belly

1 pound large shrimp, peeled and deveined

1 (8-ounce) package vermicelli rice noodles

1 (1-pound) package egg roll wrappers

1 large egg, lightly beaten

Vegetable oil, for deep frying

2 cucumbers, thinly sliced lengthwise

1 bunch Thai basil, stemmed

1 bunch mint, stemmed

1 bunch cilantro, stemmed

1 (12-ounce) package rice paper

1 bunch chives

Dipping sauce

1 teaspoon minced garlic

1 teaspoon minced shallot

2 tablespoons hoisin sauce

1 teaspoon creamy peanut butter

1 tablespoon sugar

1 tablespoon sriracha

1 teaspoon white vinegar

1. Bring a medium pot of salted water to a boil. Add the ginger, lemongrass, and pork belly and cook for 30 minutes. Transfer the pork belly to a cutting board and let it rest for 10 minutes, then slice thinly and set aside. Discard the ginger and lemongrass.

2. Bring a small pot of water to a boil. Add the shrimp and cook for 5 minutes. Transfer the shrimp to a cutting board and cut each shrimp in half lengthwise.

3. Bring a large pot of water to a boil. Add the vermicelli noodles and cook until tender, 4–5 minutes. Drain and rinse under cold water to stop the cooking process.

4. Roll each egg roll wrapper in a tight roll and seal with the beaten egg. Heat the vegetable oil in a small pot over medium heat and fry the rolled-up egg roll wrappers until golden brown, about 10 minutes.

5. To make the dipping sauce, in a small skillet, sauté the garlic and shallot over medium heat until translucent. Add the hoisin sauce, peanut butter, sugar, sriracha, and vinegar and cook until thick, 10–15 minutes.

6. Moisten 1 sheet of rice paper and lay on a cutting board. Add 2 slices of pork, a little bit of the noodles, a slice of cucumber, some of each type of herb leaves, 1 egg roll wrapper, 4 shrimp halves (pink side facing outward), and 1 chive. Roll and gently press outward away from you. Midway through the roll, fold each left and right side into the center of the spring roll and continue to roll outward to complete the roll.

7. Ladle the sauce into a small bowl for dipping.

Mom's Gifted Egg Rolls
with Pickled Daikon

Foo

When my parents immigrated to the US, they were warmly welcomed into their new community. So, every year for the holidays, my mother showed her gratitude by making dozens of egg rolls (with her kids as sous chefs), which we would package in foil and a bow to give out as gifts to the neighbors. These egg rolls, and that act of gratitude, are the reason why I cook.

This dish is packed with complex flavors and textures that are firmly bundled together. Before enjoying the egg roll, wrap it in a cool, fresh red lettuce leaf and dip it in the flavorful fish sauce. When you take your first bite, you will taste the richness of the seasoned pork, the flavors of the sea from the crab and shrimp, and the finely minced vegetables that cut through the protein. All of it is enjoyed with a side of pickled daikon to complement the egg rolls. **Serves 6**

Egg rolls

1 cup dried Chinese mushrooms

1 small head green cabbage, cored

1 small jicama, peeled

4 carrots, peeled

2 large eggs

1 pound ground pork

8 ounces shrimp, coarsely chopped

1 (6-ounce) can lump crab meat, coarsely chopped

1 (8-ounce) package vermicelli rice noodles

1 small Vidalia onion, chopped

1 bunch scallions, sliced

1 shallot, chopped

4 garlic cloves, minced

3 tablespoons fish sauce

1½ teaspoons sugar

Salt and ground black pepper to taste

1 (1-pound) package egg roll wrappers

Vegetable oil, for frying

1 head red leaf lettuce

Pickled daikon

¼ cup water

3 tablespoons white vinegar

1 tablespoon sugar

1 tablespoon salt

1 medium daikon, peeled and cut into ¼-inch cubes

Dipping sauce

2 tablespoons fish sauce

Juice of 1 lime

1½ teaspoons sugar

1 teaspoon white vinegar

1 teaspoon chili paste

½ cup water

1. In a medium bowl, soak the mushrooms in water for 15 minutes to reconstitute and soften. Drain, pat dry, and chop, then set aside.

2. With a mandoline, thinly shave and then finely chop the cabbage, jicama, and carrots. Set aside.

3. In two separate bowls, beat 1 egg and set aside.

(recipe continues)

4. In a large bowl, combine the ground pork, shrimp, crab, vermicelli, mushrooms, cabbage, jicama, carrots, Vidalia onion, scallions, shallot, garlic, 1 of the beaten eggs, the fish sauce, sugar, salt, and pepper. Mix well.

5. Lay out 1 egg roll wrapper in a diamond shape with one corner facing you. Scoop about 3 tablespoons of the egg roll filling onto the corner facing you. Begin to roll the wrapper away from you while applying a little pressure. Halfway through, fold the right and left corners into the center of the filling and continue to roll away from you. Seal the ends with some of the other beaten egg.

6. Pour the vegetable oil into a deep fryer or large, heavy-bottomed pot and heat to 300 degrees F. Set a wire rack over a rimmed baking sheet.

7. Add 3 egg rolls at a time to the hot oil and fry until golden brown, about 7 minutes. Transfer to the prepared rack.

8. To make the pickled daikon, in a medium bowl, whisk together the water, vinegar, sugar, and salt to make a quick brine. Add the cubed daikon.

9. To make the dipping sauce, combine the fish sauce, lime juice, sugar, vinegar, chili paste, and water in a small bowl and stir until the sugar is dissolved.

10. Serve the egg rolls with lettuce leaves for wrapping. Offer the pickled daikon and dipping sauce alongside.

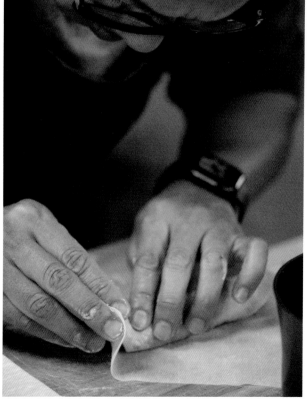

Mandu

Pot Stickers

Tony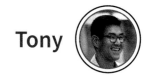

To put it simply, I love pot stickers. From the Chinese takeout staple to homemade dumplings, whether they are pan-fried, steamed, or deep-fried, they scream nostalgia, instantly reminding me of home and making me happy. I am adopted, and my family would have them on my "Arrival Day"—the anniversary of the first day I joined my family in the US—accompanied by Beef Bulgogi with Quick Pickled Vegetables (page 137). These are Korean-style pot stickers filled with vegetables and spices and served with dipping sauce. **Serves 6**

Pot stickers

1 pound ground pork

1 cup kimchi, drained and chopped

1 cup finely chopped napa cabbage

½ cup minced white or brown mushrooms

½ cup finely chopped scallions, plus more for garnish

4 garlic cloves, minced

1 (2-inch) knob ginger, grated

1 large egg, lightly beaten

1½ tablespoons toasted sesame oil

1 tablespoon hot chili oil or garlic chili sauce

1 tablespoon soy sauce

2 teaspoons gochujang

1 tablespoon gochugaru (Korean red pepper flakes)

1 tablespoon sesame seeds

1 teaspoon sugar

½ teaspoon salt

½ teaspoon ground black pepper

1 (14- to 16-ounce) package dumpling wrappers

3 tablespoons vegetable oil, divided

1 cup water

Dipping sauce

2 tablespoons soy sauce

1 tablespoon rice wine vinegar

1 tablespoon toasted sesame oil

2 garlic cloves, minced, or 1 teaspoon garlic powder

½ teaspoon salt

½ teaspoon ground black pepper

1 teaspoon sesame seeds

2 scallions, thinly sliced

1. To make the dipping sauce, in a small bowl, whisk together the soy sauce, vinegar, sesame oil, garlic, salt, pepper, sesame seeds, and scallions. Set aside.

2. In a large bowl, combine the pork, kimchi, cabbage, mushrooms, scallions, garlic, ginger, egg, sesame oil, hot chili oil, soy sauce, gochujang, gochugaru, sesame seeds, sugar, salt, and pepper. Mix thoroughly and make sure everything is incorporated. Pinch off a small portion and cook it in a small skillet for a couple minutes, until fully cooked. Taste and make sure the mixture is seasoned appropriately; adjust seasoning as needed.

3. Have a small bowl of water ready while you fill the dumplings. Working with one dumpling wrapper at a time, place a generous tablespoon of the mixture in the center of the wrapper. Dip one finger in the water and run it along the edge of the wrapper. Crimp the edges shut, making sure there is

(recipe continues)

no air in the dumpling and all the edges are sealed tight. (If you like, you can work on your pleating technique and shape the pot sticker into a half-moon.) Place the finished dumpling on a rimmed baking sheet. Continue until all the wrappers and filling are used up.

4. Heat 1 tablespoon of the vegetable oil in a large skillet over medium-high heat. Place dumplings in a circle, filling the pan but not crowding it. Cook until the bottoms are starting to brown and crisp up, 4–6 minutes. Pour in ⅓ cup of the water and cover the skillet. Steam/fry the dumplings until the water is evaporated and the dumplings are cooked through, another 4–5 minutes. Repeat, using more oil and water, to cook the remaining dumplings.

5. Place the dumplings in a shallow bowl or plate, garnish with scallions, and serve the dipping sauce on the side.

Lola's Lumpia Shanghai

Leah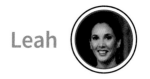

In the Philippines, we have two kinds of spring rolls, or as we call them, Lumpia, fresh and fried. The fresh version has an almost crepe-like wrapper. While those are delicious, it's the fried version, lumpia Shanghai, that always puts a smile on my face. My parents say that's been true since I was a toddler. Now I get to watch as my son falls in love with them too. They are a staple at every Filipino party, holiday, and birthday. These can be filled with whatever combination of beef, pork, or vegetables you like. The combination in this recipe is my favorite. **Makes 15 rolls**

---

4 ounces ground beef

8 ounces ground pork

6 garlic cloves, finely chopped

2 tablespoons finely chopped ginger

½ cup water chestnuts, rinsed, drained, and cut into small dice

¼ cup finely diced carrot

½ small Spanish onion, finely diced

3 tablespoons low-sodium soy sauce

¾ teaspoon toasted sesame oil

1 teaspoon kosher salt

½ teaspoon ground black pepper

1 scallion, thinly sliced

1 large egg

1 tablespoon water

15 spring roll wrappers

Peanut or vegetable oil, for deep frying

1½ cups sweet chili sauce

---

1. Put the beef and pork in a large bowl and gently mix to combine. Add the garlic, ginger, water chestnuts, carrot, onion, soy sauce, sesame oil, salt, pepper, and scallion and mix until combined.

2. Line a rimmed baking sheet with parchment paper. In a small bowl, whisk together the egg and water.

3. Separate the spring roll wrappers and cover them with a damp paper towel to prevent them from drying out. Place a wrapper on your work surface so that a point is facing you. Place about 2 heaping tablespoons of the filling on the wrapper and spread it out to the edges. Turn up the bottom corner and roll upward. Fold in the left and right corners, making sure the filling is nicely packed, with no air pockets. Continue rolling. Dip your finger in the egg wash, pat it on the remaining corner, and finish rolling the lumpia, sealing the edge.

4. Put the lumpia on the lined baking sheet. Repeat to make the remaining lumpia. The lumpia can be made to this point and refrigerated, covered with a damp towel, for up to 8 hours, or frozen in an airtight container.

5. Heat the peanut oil in a wok or Dutch oven over medium heat until it reaches 350 degrees F. Line another baking sheet with paper towels. Fry the lumpia in batches of 4–6, until golden brown and crispy and cooked through, about 4 minutes for fresh lumpia or 6 minutes for frozen. Use a slotted spoon to transfer to the paper towels. Serve with sweet chili sauce on the side.

Spicy Fried Chicken Drumettes

I grew up in the Midwest and love fried chicken. This side of spicy, crispy double-fried chicken drumettes is a classic American food with my own spin: the chicken is dressed in garlic powder and fish sauce and topped with Thai peppers and cilantro to bring heat and herbal flavors. In the final challenge of *The Great American Recipe*, I served these chicken drumettes alongside my Pork Noodle Soup (page 43), representing my Vietnamese American upbringing on a plate. **Serves 6**

---

4 tablespoons fish sauce, divided

1 tablespoon rice wine

1 tablespoon chicken bouillon powder

1 tablespoon salt

2 teaspoons garlic powder, divided

1 teaspoon ground black pepper

2 pounds chicken drumettes

Juice of 2 limes

2 tablespoons rice vinegar

2 tablespoons sugar

3 tablespoons fried shallots

4 garlic cloves, minced

7 Thai red peppers, chopped

6 jalapeños, chopped

2 cups cornstarch

1 tablespoon baking powder

Vegetable oil, for deep frying

3 tablespoons finely chopped fresh cilantro

---

1. In a large bowl, whisk together 1 tablespoon of the fish sauce, the rice wine, chicken bouillon, salt, 1 teaspoon of the garlic powder, and the pepper. Add the drumettes and toss to coat. Cover and refrigerate for 20 minutes.

2. In a small saucepan, combine the lime juice, vinegar, remaining 3 tablespoons fish sauce, and sugar. Cook over medium heat, stirring until all the sugar is dissolved, 8–10 minutes. Remove from the heat.

3. In another small saucepan, sauté the fried shallots, garlic, Thai peppers, and jalapeños over medium heat until the garlic is slightly brown, about 10 minutes. Remove from the heat.

4. Remove the chicken from the refrigerator. In a separate bowl, whisk together the cornstarch, baking powder, and remaining 1 teaspoon garlic powder. Dredge the drumettes in the mixture.

5. Pour the oil into a deep fryer or large, heavy-bottomed pot and heat to 275 degrees F. Set a wire rack over a rimmed baking sheet.

6. Add 4–5 drumettes at a time to the hot oil and fry until brown and cooked through, about 10 minutes. Transfer to the prepared rack.

7. Increase the oil temperature to 350 degrees F. Return the drumettes to the hot oil, fry for an additional 3–5 minutes, and place on the rack again.

8. Transfer all the chicken to a large bowl, add the cooked fish sauce, sautéed garlic and peppers, and cilantro, and toss well. Serve hot.

Mofongo con Camarones

Mofongo with Shrimp

Irma

Mofongo is one of those dishes that you just can't stop eating! It is the equivalent of Southern comfort food to the Caribbean, and it is the perfect marriage of Puerto Rican and Dominican cuisine. Though both cultures like to lay claim to this dish as their own, it is largely recognized as a Puerto Rican dish of western African origin. The dish of fried unripe plantains is traditionally made with chicharron (pork rinds/cracklings), but I prefer it without them; this is my take, and you can easily make mofongo all your own. Note: Peeling green plantains can be challenging, especially if you've never done it before. I recommend searching online for a how-to video. **Serves 6**

5–6 green plantains

4 tablespoons (½ stick) salted butter

1 pound large shrimp, peeled and deveined (set aside 12 shrimp with tails left on for garnish)

½ cup olive oil, plus more for drizzling

Salt and ground black pepper to taste

½ bunch cilantro, chopped

1½ cups chicken broth, divided

Vegetable oil, for deep frying

6 garlic cloves, peeled

Juice of 1 lime

---

1. First, peel and slice your plantains. Cut off both ends of each plantain. Then, with the tip of your knife, cut a shallow slice down the length of the plantains at each ridge. Slide the tip of your knife between the plantain flesh and the peel to loosen, then remove the peels in strips. Slice your plantains into 1½-inch-thick pieces, then set aside.

2. Melt the butter in a large skillet over medium heat. Add the shrimp, drizzle with olive oil, season with salt and pepper, and add most of your chopped cilantro (reserve some cilantro for garnish). Cook until the shrimp are opaque and just cooked through, 1–2 minutes per side, then transfer to a plate to cool.

3. To make the sauce, add 1 cup of the chicken broth to the pan, turn the heat down to low, and bring to a simmer. Taste and adjust for seasoning, then cover to keep warm.

4. Pour the vegetable oil into a deep fryer or large, heavy-bottomed pot and heat to 350 degrees F. Add the plantains and fry, turning them after a couple of minutes, 3–4 minutes on each side. Check for doneness with a fork. You are looking for a nice golden color and your plantains to be cooked all the way through. You don't want to fry your green plantains too fast or hard—make sure they cook completely but don't become too crisp to mash. Once your plantains are fried, set aside on paper towels to drain.

5. Mash the garlic cloves in a mortar and pestle—no cheating! This is the traditional way and the only way to make mofongo. Put the mashed garlic in a bowl, add the olive oil and remaining ½ cup chicken broth, and season with salt and pepper. Set aside.

6. Reserve 12 whole shrimp for garnish, then cut the remaining shrimp into small pieces.

7. Mash the fried plantains, 5 or 6 pieces at a time depending on the size of your mortar, with some of the broth-oil mixture, so that your mofongo is not dry. Transfer to a plate or bowl and mash in some of the shrimp pieces. Continue until you have mashed all of the plantains and shrimp.

8. Fill six small ramekins with the mashed plantain and shrimp mixture and invert them onto small serving plates. Drizzle the pan sauce on and around the mofongo. Garnish each serving with 2 reserved tail-on shrimp and some cilantro, then drizzle fresh lime juice over the top.

Rhode Island–Style Fried Calamari

Dan

I have lived in or around Providence, Rhode Island, my whole life, surrounded by its fresh seafood. Battered squid tossed with hot cherry peppers is a great representation of where I live and of my Italian roots. My family loves this recipe and has been making it for many generations. **Serves 12**

---

3 pounds large squid, cleaned, tubes sliced into 1-inch pieces and tentacles left whole

4 cups buttermilk

Vegetable oil, for deep frying

1 tablespoon olive oil

2 tablespoons salted butter

3 garlic cloves, minced

1 (16-ounce) jar sliced banana peppers, drained

1 (16-ounce) jar sliced hot cherry peppers, drained and 1½ tablespoons juice reserved

¼ teaspoon garlic powder

3 cups all-purpose batter mix, such as Fis-Chic

¼ teaspoon ground black pepper

¼ teaspoon kosher salt

Chopped fresh flat-leaf parsley, for garnish

3 lemons, cut into wedges (see note)

1 (1-pound) package mesclun mix

---

1. In a large bowl, soak the squid in the buttermilk for 20 minutes.

2. Pour the vegetable oil into a deep fryer or large, heavy-bottomed pot and heat to 375 degrees F.

3. Meanwhile, heat the olive oil and butter in a large skillet over low heat. Add the garlic and cook until just browned, then add the banana peppers, cherry peppers, reserved pepper juice, and garlic powder and cook just until heated through. Set aside.

4. Put the batter mix in a large bowl. Drain the squid and coat it in the batter mix.

5. Working in batches as necessary, add the squid to the hot oil and fry for 3 minutes, seasoning with the black pepper while it fries.

6. Transfer the calamari to paper towels, season with the salt, and let drain for 1 minute, then transfer to a large bowl. When all the calamari is done, quickly toss with the pepper mixture.

7. Pour the calamari and peppers onto a platter, sprinkle with parsley, and serve with lemon wedges and mesclun mix.

Note: Instead of cutting the lemon into wedges, you can make 45-degree cuts all around each lemon to cut it in half, then dip the lemon halves into the parsley.

Bacalaitos

Fish Fritters

Irma

This dish is a staple in my home. We always have fish stocked in the freezer. Wild-caught pollock fritters are a delicious and easy snack for when the kids show up unexpectedly, or even a light meal for when you've had a long day and don't want to put together an elaborate dinner. Who doesn't like something fried?

Traditionally, bacalaitos are made with salted cod, but you have to soak it in water for hours just to remove the excess salt. This technique came all the way from Spain; salt was used to preserve the cod carried over on slave boats coming into the Americas. Pollock is a wonderful substitute because it is more affordable and significantly shortens the prep time for your bacalaitos. Feel free to use another mild white fish if you like. **Serves 6**

1 pound pollock fillets

2 cups all-purpose flour

2 teaspoons baking powder or cornstarch (see notes)

1 teaspoon minced garlic

1 tablespoon garlic powder

1 tablespoon onion powder

1 teaspoon ground annatto (achiote powder) (see notes)

1 teaspoon ground coriander

1 teaspoon dried oregano

¼ teaspoon ground turmeric

Salt and ground black pepper to taste

Chopped fresh cilantro to taste

Vegetable oil, for deep frying

¼ cup ketchup

¼ cup mayonnaise

Juice of ½ lemon

1 teaspoon chopped fresh flat-leaf parsley

1. Bring a large pot of water to a boil. Add the fish and boil until cooked through, about 8 minutes. Drain, reserving 2 cups of the cooking water. Transfer the cooked fish to a cutting board.

2. In a large bowl, combine the flour, baking powder, garlic, garlic powder, onion powder, annatto, coriander, oregano, turmeric, salt, and pepper and mix well.

3. Using a simple fork, shred the fish and add it to the bowl with the seasoned flour. Stir in the reserved 2 cups cooking water along with the fresh cilantro and mix well.

4. Pour the oil into a deep fryer or large, heavy-bottomed pot and heat to 350 degrees F. Working in batches, add a few large spoonfuls of the fish mixture to the hot oil and fry until golden on both sides, turning once, 2–3 minutes per side, or a bit longer if you like crispier fritters. Transfer to paper towels to drain. Do not overlay, as they will get greasy.

5. To make the dipping sauce, in a small bowl, combine the ketchup, mayonnaise, lemon juice, and parsley. Mix well.

6. Serve the bacalaitos hot with the dipping sauce.

Notes: Baking powder in the batter makes a thicker coating for your fritters. If you prefer your coating thin and crispy, omit the baking powder or substitute an equal amount of cornstarch. The color of your bacalaitos will depend on your ground annatto, also known as achiote powder. When I make these at home, they come out golden brown, but on *The Great American Recipe* I was surprised when an unfamiliar brand of annatto turned my bacalaitos fiery red! They still tasted delicious, though.

Spinach–Stuffed Squid over Rainbow Chard

Robin

A large Calabrian family moved to my hometown of Annapolis and became my second family. We would have an annual weekend gathering preceded by three days of cooking together. This brought a lot of new recipes into my mother's kitchen, including these whimsically stuffed squid with their tentacles that always attracted my mother's eye for unique techniques. This dish is so very delicious, it will transport you and your family to the seaside. **Serves 6**

1½ pounds squid, tentacles and body separated

Grated zest and juice of 2 lemons, plus wedges for garnish

Salt to taste

8 tablespoons olive oil, divided

1 pound spinach

1 large shallot, finely chopped

4 garlic cloves, minced

2 flat-leaf parsley sprigs, plus additional chopped parsley for garnish

4 canned anchovy fillets

1 teaspoon dried thyme

1 teaspoon dried oregano

Pinch red pepper flakes

¼ cup panko bread crumbs

½ cup mayonnaise

1 cup dry white wine

1 large bunch rainbow chard, stemmed and chopped

1. Pat the squid dry and place it in a large baking dish. Drizzle the lemon juice over the squid and season with salt.

2. Heat 2 tablespoons of the olive oil in a large skillet over medium heat. Add the spinach and heat just long enough to wilt, about 1 minute. Use tongs to transfer the spinach to a plate.

3. Add another 2 tablespoons olive oil to the same skillet and add the shallot, garlic, parsley sprigs, anchovies, thyme, oregano, and red pepper flakes. Cook for 2 minutes, then transfer to the plate with the spinach.

4. Put the spinach and anchovy mixture, along with the lemon zest, in a food processor and puree. Add the panko and pulse a few times.

5. With a tiny spoon, fill the squid tubes with the spinach-anchovy filling and close the tops with a toothpick. Brush a little mayonnaise across the outside of each stuffed squid. Cut the tentacles into long pieces, with only a few suckers intact per piece.

6. Heat the remaining 4 tablespoons olive oil in a large cast iron skillet over medium-high heat. Add the stuffed squid and brown lightly, then turn them over and add the tentacles and wine. As soon as the tentacles change color, transfer them to a platter. Cover the skillet and cook until the squid is firm, about 1 minute. Uncover the skillet, season the squid with salt, and cook for another minute. Use a slotted spoon to transfer the squid to the platter.

7. Add the rainbow chard to the liquid remaining in the skillet and heat just enough to wilt, then remove the skillet from the heat.

8. Place some chard on each appetizer plate. Add several stuffed squid on top, then scatter some tentacles around the plate. Garnish with fresh parsley and a drizzle of the reduced liquid in the skillet. Serve with lemon wedges on the side for squeezing.

Southern Smoke Mac and Cheese

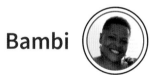
Bambi

Mac and cheese is a staple of Southern soul food. Every family has their own version! Passed down through the generations of my family, this recipe has been updated with my signature twists: smoked Gouda cheese and smoked paprika, which add smoky flair to a crowd-pleasing classic side dish. This dish celebrates Southern traditions and is an expression of gratitude for the many evolutions of Southern cooking. **Serves 8**

Softened unsalted butter, for greasing

2 teaspoons chicken bouillon powder

1 pound elbow macaroni

1½ cups evaporated milk

2 (4-ounce) cheese sauce packets, such as Velveeta

1 teaspoon salt-free seasoning blend, such as Dash

½ teaspoon ground black pepper

½ teaspoon ground mustard

½ teaspoon onion powder

½ teaspoon garlic powder

¼ teaspoon sugar, or to taste

1 large egg, lightly beaten

2 cups shredded Monterey Jack cheese

2 cups shredded Colby cheese

2 cups shredded sharp cheddar cheese, divided

1 cup smoked Gouda cheese

8 thick slices bacon, cooked until crisp and crumbled

1 teaspoon smoked paprika, divided

1 jalapeño, seeded and finely minced, for garnish

1. Preheat the oven to 400 degrees F. Have ready a large, deep glass baking dish or small individual crocks. Grease the baking dish or crocks with softened butter.

2. Fill a large pot with water, add the chicken bouillon, and bring to a rolling boil. Add the pasta and cook for 10 minutes. Drain and set aside.

3. In a saucepan, combine the evaporated milk, cheese sauce, seasoning blend, pepper, mustard, onion powder, garlic powder, and sugar and heat over medium-low heat. Mix well. Add the egg and keep stirring so the sauce doesn't burn.

4. Pour the pasta into the prepared baking dish and add the cheese sauce, Monterey Jack cheese, Colby cheese, and 1 cup of the cheddar cheese. Mix well until evenly distributed. Or, to make individual crocks of mac and cheese, add the pasta to the pot with the cheese sauce and stir in the Monterey Jack cheese, Colby cheese, and 1 cup of the cheddar. Mix well and divide between the prepared crocks.

5. Cover the top of the mac and cheese mixture in the baking dish or crocks with the smoked Gouda cheese, remaining 1 cup cheddar cheese, crumbled bacon, and ½ teaspoon of the smoked paprika. Cover with aluminum foil and bake for 25 minutes (or 15 minutes for individual crocks). Uncover and bake for another 5 minutes, or until the top is golden brown. Sprinkle the remaining ½ teaspoon smoked paprika on top. Garnish with the jalapeño and serve.

Baked Stuffed Quahogs

Dan

I grew up in a close-knit Italian community in Rhode Island. One day, a neighbor and I started talking, and we discovered—and bonded over—our shared love of seafood. He gave me this recipe for stuffed quahogs. Quahogs are large clams found in the region I grew up and live in, and I would spend hours harvesting quahogs on the beach to make this recipe, so for me, it's as local as it gets. I cook this recipe twice a year: on Christmas Eve and on my mother's birthday, because this is her favorite dish. **Serves 6**

9 large quahogs or hard clams

3 sleeves Ritz crackers

¼ cup canned crushed tomatoes

2 tablespoons olive oil

1 tablespoon hot sauce, such as Frank's RedHot

1 tablespoon chopped fresh flat-leaf parsley

¼ teaspoon onion powder

¼ teaspoon garlic powder

3 lemons, cut into wedges

1. Preheat the oven to 400 degrees F.

2. Shuck the quahogs over a bowl to catch the juice. Reserve the shells.

3. Roughly chop the quahogs, but do not mince them.

4. In a large bowl, crush the Ritz crackers into coarse pieces, but do not let them turn to dust. There should still be noticeable pieces of cracker. Add ½ cup of the reserved quahog juice, the tomatoes, olive oil, hot sauce, parsley, onion powder, and garlic powder and mix well. Add the quahogs and mix. Spoon the mixture into the shell halves.

5. Place the stuffed quahogs on a rimmed baking sheet and bake for 20–25 minutes, or until golden brown on top. Serve with lemon wedges.

Linguiça Beans

Silvia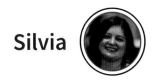

These beans feature Portuguese linguiça, a delicious sausage introduced to me by our dear compadre Frank, who is *padrino* (godfather) to my son. These beans are inspired both by frijoles charros, a traditional Mexican dish made with beans, tomatoes, onions, peppers, and a combination of meat, as well as by the large population of Portuguese Americans who live in San Luis Obispo, California, many of whom trace their origins to the Azores. Their food has enriched my own on many levels. These linguiça beans cook at a low temperature for a long time to create a rich, deep flavor, which is a great pairing for my Beef Parrillada Tacos (page 84) or Tri-Tip Tacos (page 82). **Serves 6**

---

1 teaspoon vegetable oil

11 ounces spicy Portuguese linguiça sausage, removed from casings and chopped

1 white onion, chopped

8 ounces Roma tomatoes, chopped

2 garlic cloves, minced

3 (16-ounce) cans pinto beans, drained and rinsed

1 bunch cilantro, chopped, a few leaves reserved for garnish

1–2 cups water

Salt and ground black pepper to taste

---

1. Heat the oil in a Dutch oven over high heat. Add the linguiça and cook until soft, about 10 minutes.

2. Add the onion, tomatoes, and garlic and cook until soft, about 3 minutes.

3. Add the pinto beans, cilantro, and water (start with 1 cup of water and add more, up to 2 cups, until the soup reaches your desired consistency). Season with salt and pepper. Cover, turn the heat down to low, and cook for 30 minutes. Garnish with cilantro and serve.

Note: *Pictured on page 84*

Kimchi Fried Rice

Tony

I always have a jar of kimchi, some leftover cooked white rice, and a bottle of soy sauce in the fridge. Spicy, flavorful, and packed with vegetables, this is my go-to dish when I'm hungry and need something quick. This dish can be served as a side or an entrée, and you can make it your own by adding in any protein you like—or what you have available in your fridge and need to use up. **Serves 4**

⅓ cup gochujang

2 tablespoons hot chili oil or garlic chili sauce, plus more for garnish

2 tablespoons soy sauce

2 teaspoons toasted sesame oil

½ teaspoon salt

½ teaspoon ground black pepper

2–3 tablespoons vegetable oil, divided

4–5 tablespoons (½ stick) unsalted butter, divided

1 (2-inch) knob ginger, grated

5 garlic cloves, minced

1 carrot, peeled and diced

1 red bell pepper, seeded and diced

½ white onion, diced

3 scallions, chopped, plus more for garnish

1½ cups kimchi, drained and chopped

2 cups cold, leftover cooked white rice

4 large eggs

Black and white sesame seeds, for garnish (optional)

Furikake, for garnish (optional)

---

1. In a bowl, whisk together the gochujang, chili oil, soy sauce, sesame oil, salt, and pepper. Set aside.

2. In a large skillet or wok, heat 1–2 tablespoons of the vegetable oil and 1–2 tablespoons of the butter over medium-high heat. Add the ginger and garlic and cook until fragrant, about 1 minute. Add the carrot, bell pepper, onion, scallions, and kimchi and sauté for 3–4 minutes. Add the gochujang mixture and cook for 2 minutes. Add the rice and toss until everything is evenly distributed and heated through, 3–4 minutes. You want the rice to get some caramelized crunchy parts. Add the remaining 3 tablespoons butter and stir until melted and incorporated.

3. In a small skillet, heat the remaining 1 tablespoon vegetable oil over medium-low heat. Fry the eggs until done to your liking.

4. Serve the kimchi fried rice in bowls with a fried egg on top. Garnish with chopped scallions, chili oil, sesame seeds, and furikake.

Fried Zucchini Flowers

Tiffany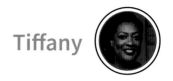

My family had a farm and we had an abundance of vegetables on the table for every meal. Growing zucchini brings an extra bonus: their edible flowers, which are in season in early summer. If you don't grow your own, look for zucchini flowers at farmers' markets. **Serves 4–6**

Batter

2 cups all-purpose flour

½ cup cornstarch

1 tablespoon baking powder

1 tablespoon salt

½ teaspoon Creole seasoning

2¼ cups light beer

¼ cup ice-cold vodka

Mozzarella filling

8 ounces fresh mozzarella, finely diced

3 anchovy fillets, minced

3 basil leaves, minced

Grated zest of ½ lemon

Salt and ground black pepper to taste

Zucchini blossoms

Cornstarch, for dusting

12 zucchini blossoms

Vegetable oil, for deep frying

1. To make the batter, in a medium bowl, whisk together the flour, cornstarch, baking powder, salt, and Creole seasoning. Add the beer, then the vodka, whisking well to combine.

2. To make the mozzarella stuffing, in a small bowl, combine the mozzarella, anchovies, basil, lemon zest, and salt and pepper. Toss well to combine.

3. Put some cornstarch in a shallow dish or pie plate for dusting.

4. Remove and discard the center bulb from the inside of each zucchini blossom. Fill each blossom with about 1 tablespoon of the mozzarella mixture and reclose. Dredge the blossoms in the cornstarch and roll them to coat well.

5. Pour the oil into a large, heavy-bottomed pot and heat to 350 degrees F.

6. Dunk each blossom in the batter, allowing the excess to drip back into the bowl. Working in batches as necessary, fry the blossoms until golden brown, about 2 minutes, then use a slotted spoon to transfer to paper towels to drain. Serve warm.

Soups, Stews,
and Salads

Spicy Cauliflower Zuppa Toscana 39

Sopa Tarasca 40

Green Pozole 42

Pork Noodle Soup 43

Pasta e Fagioli 47
(Pasta and Bean Soup)

Bun Rieu 48
(Vietnamese Pork and Crab Meatball Soup)

Mrs. Nguyen's Pho 50

Chloe's Halftime: Vietnamese Beef Stew 53

Moqueca and Pão de Queijo 55
(Brazilian Seafood Stew and Cheese Bread)

Cioppino 57

Beet, Fig, and Pine Nut Salad in Endive 59

**Spring Pea Salad with Preserved Lemon
and Celery Seed Vinaigrette** 61

Grilled Calamari Mango Salad 62

Steak Salad 63

Spicy Cauliflower Zuppa Toscana

Brian

with Crusty Garlic Bread

This spicy soup is the perfect meal for cold weather—rain, snow, or just the way the wind blows. Surprisingly light, the soup will warm your insides without sending you into a food coma. The cauliflower soaks up every bit of flavor in the pot, just like the crusty bread will sop up every drop of soup in the bottom of your bowl. **Serves 4**

Soup

1 pound spicy breakfast sausage, casings removed

1 pound bacon, cut into 1-inch pieces

1 medium onion, chopped

4 garlic cloves, minced

3 cups chopped spinach leaves

1 teaspoon red pepper flakes

1 whole cauliflower head, broken into florets

4 cups chicken broth

½ cup heavy cream

Salt and ground black pepper to taste

Bread

1 baguette or other loaf of crusty bread, sliced open horizontally

Olive oil, for drizzling

1 head garlic

¼ cup grated Parmesan cheese

1. In a large pot, cook the sausage over medium-high heat until browned, 10–12 minutes. Transfer the sausage to a paper towel–lined plate to drain.

2. Add the bacon to the fat remaining in the pot and cook until crisp. Transfer to the same plate as the sausage.

3. Pour off all but 2 tablespoons fat from the pot. Add the onion and cook until translucent, about 5 minutes. Add the garlic, spinach, and red pepper flakes and cook until the spinach is wilted, about 2 minutes.

4. Add the sausage, bacon, and cauliflower florets to the pot, pour in the chicken broth, and simmer for about 20 minutes. Stir in the cream and cook for another 10 minutes. Season with salt and pepper.

5. When the soup is nearly done, turn on the oven broiler. Coat the cut sides of the bread halves with olive oil. Broil until golden brown. Cut the head of garlic in half and rub it all over the crusty bread. Cut the bread crosswise into slices.

6. Generously ladle the soup into bowls, making sure to get all the bits and bobs, and top with a sprinkling of Parmesan cheese. Serve with bread for dunking.

Sopa Tarasca

Silvia

A simple yet elegant traditional soup from the Mexican state of Michoacán, sopa tarasca features prominently on nearly every restaurant menu in the state. The soup is made from beans, tomatoes, and dried ancho chiles, which give it body and depth of flavor. What make it sing are the crunchy, creamy, colorful garnishes on top. This dish is balanced and delicious! **Serves 4**

3 Roma tomatoes

½ medium white onion

2 garlic cloves, peeled

4 ancho peppers

3 cups chicken broth, divided

4 teaspoons salt, plus more to taste

8 tablespoons vegetable oil, divided

2 teaspoons dried Mexican oregano

2 (16-ounce) cans no-salt-added pinto beans, drained and rinsed

½ teaspoon ground black pepper

10 (6-inch) corn tortillas, cut into long, thin strips

1 large ripe avocado

10 ounces cotija cheese, cut into small dice

Cilantro sprigs, for garnish

Crema Mexicana (Mexican-style sour cream) to taste

1. In a cast iron skillet or comal, roast the tomatoes, onion, and garlic over medium-high heat, turning often, until soft, 10–12 minutes.

2. Cut one of the ancho peppers in half and roast one half in the skillet for a few seconds per side, just enough to release the aroma. Transfer it to a small bowl, cover with boiling water, and let it rehydrate for 10 minutes, then drain.

3. Put the tomatoes, onion, garlic, rehydrated ancho half, 1 cup of the broth, and ½ teaspoon of the salt in a blender and blend until smooth.

4. In a Dutch oven, heat 2 tablespoons of the oil over medium heat. Strain the tomato sauce into the hot oil, add the oregano, cover, and simmer for 5 minutes.

5. Put the beans and the remaining 2 cups broth in the blender and blend until smooth. Add the bean puree to the tomato sauce. Season with the black pepper. Bring to a boil, then lower the heat to medium-high, cover, and cook for 15 minutes. Taste and adjust the salt and pepper if needed.

6. While the soup is cooking, seed and thinly slice the remaining ancho peppers and set aside.

7. Line a plate with paper towels. Heat the remaining oil in a skillet over high heat and fry the tortilla strips in batches. Don't crowd the pot and don't take your eyes off them because they fry fast. Transfer to the paper towels and immediately season the tortillas with salt.

8. Place the sliced ancho peppers in a spider strainer and submerge it in the oil for no more than 3 seconds (they burn easily). Transfer to a plate and immediately season with salt. Set aside.

9. When ready to serve, peel, pit, and dice the avocado. Serve the soup in bowls, topped with the fried tortillas, fried ancho peppers, cotija, avocado, and a cilantro sprig. Drizzle with crema Mexicana and serve immediately.

Green Pozole

Silvia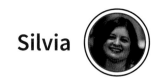

This green pozole is a very important dish to me, not only because it is a cherished family recipe, but because it became so popular on my blog, it changed the trajectory of my career and life. A very popular Mexican dish, pozole is a soup made with hominy, peppers, and meat and garnished with crisp vegetables. The pozole I grew up eating was red pozole made with pork. Later, my mom changed the recipe, replacing the pork with chicken and the red salsa with green salsa. **Serves 8–10**

---

2 (25-ounce) cans Mexican-style hominy, drained and rinsed

1 small whole chicken, cut into serving pieces

1 head garlic, plus 2 additional peeled garlic cloves

10–12 cups water

¼ medium white onion, left whole, plus 1 medium white onion, chopped

1 pound tomatillos

2 serrano peppers

1 large bunch cilantro

1 tablespoon dried Mexican oregano, plus more for serving

1 tablespoon salt, plus more to taste

3 large avocados

1 head iceberg lettuce, sliced

1 bunch red radishes, sliced

5 limes, cut in half

16–20 tostada shells

---

1. In a large pot, combine the hominy, chicken, and whole garlic head. Pour in enough water to cover everything (about 10 cups). Bring to a boil, then reduce the heat and simmer for 40 minutes, or until the chicken is fully cooked. Transfer the chicken to a plate to cool. Remove the garlic head from the broth and squeeze the soft garlic out of their skins and into the broth.

2. In a blender, combine 1 cup water, the remaining 2 garlic cloves, ¼ onion, tomatillos, serrano peppers, cilantro, oregano, and salt and blend until smooth.

3. Add the tomatillo mixture to the pot and simmer for 20 minutes over low heat.

4. Shred the cooked chicken, discarding the skin and bones, and return the meat to the pot. Mix well. Taste and add more salt if needed.

5. When ready to serve, peel, pit, and slice the avocados.

6. Serve the pozole in bowls, garnished with the chopped onion, lettuce, radishes, avocado, oregano, and lime halves for squeezing, with tostadas on the side.

Pork Noodle Soup

I was raised eating noodles, a staple in every Vietnamese household. Noodles, more than any other food, represent my childhood. This soup really packs umami flavors in the rich pork stock, while the grilled shrimp and fresh herbs contrast with the broth, creating a spoonful of silky balance. I am so happy to share this recipe with you. It truly is my Great American Recipe. **Serves 6**

Pickled onions

¼ cup white vinegar

¼ cup rice vinegar

½ cup water

¼ cup sugar

½ teaspoon kosher salt

1 red onion, thinly sliced

Soup

1 rack pork spareribs, cut into 3-inch riblets

5 tablespoons plus 1 teaspoon fish sauce

3 tablespoons minced garlic

3 tablespoons fried shallots

1 tablespoon Chinese rock sugar (see note on page 54)

Salt and ground black pepper to taste

4 cups chicken broth

3 cups water

1 tablespoon olive oil

9 large tiger shrimp

3 dried cuttlefish (see note)

1 (8-ounce) package dried rice vermicelli noodles, cooked according to package instructions

Broth

8 cups water

4 cups chicken broth

2 tablespoons chicken bouillon powder

2 tablespoons shrimp paste

2 tablespoons Chinese rock sugar (see note on page 54)

1 tablespoon whole black peppercorns

Garnish

8 ounces bean sprouts

1 bunch scallions, sliced

1 bunch cilantro, leaves picked

1 bunch Thai basil, leaves picked

1 bunch sawtooth coriander, leaves picked

1 bunch purple perilla, leaves picked

3 tablespoons fried shallots

6 limes, cut into wedges

1. To make the pickled onions, combine the white vinegar, rice vinegar, water, sugar, and salt in a bowl and stir until the sugar and salt dissolve. Add the red onion and stir. Cover and refrigerate for 30 minutes.

2. Combine the spareribs, 5 tablespoons of the fish sauce, garlic, fried shallots, rock sugar, salt, pepper, chicken broth, and water in a pressure cooker. Cook on high pressure for 30 minutes.

3. Meanwhile, preheat a grill. In a bowl, combine the olive oil, remaining 1 teaspoon fish sauce, salt, and pepper. Add the shrimp and toss to coat. Grill for 2–3 minutes per side. Grill the cuttlefish until they are slightly tender and charred, 3–4 minutes per side. Peel and devein the shrimp, leaving the tails on. Set the shrimp and cuttlefish aside.

4. Meanwhile, make the broth. In a large pot, combine the water, chicken broth, chicken bouillon, shrimp paste, rock sugar, and peppercorns and bring to a rapid boil. Turn down the heat to low, cover the pot, and cook for 20 minutes. Strain the broth.

(recipe continues)

5. When the pressure cooker is finished, add the strained broth to the pressure cooker. Cook on medium heat for 10 minutes.

6. Divide the vermicelli into soup bowls. Add the ribs and grilled shrimp and cuttlefish. Ladle the hot broth into the bowls and garnish each serving with bean sprouts, scallions, herbs, fried shallots, pickled onions, and lime wedges.

Note: Look for dried cuttlefish in the international aisle of your grocery store or online. Be sure you are buying whole dried cuttlefish; it is sometimes sold shredded as a snack.

Spicy Fried Chicken Drumettes
(page 18) are also pictured

Pasta e Fagioli
Pasta and Bean Soup

Dan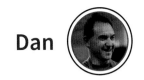

Every Wednesday, my grandma made this pork, bean, and pasta soup for a family meal. It was a family tradition, and making this recipe, which she passed down to me, always reminds me of my grandma and of many meals with loved ones. I hope to honor the tradition of sharing that I grew up with by sharing this dish with you. **Serves 4**

2 tablespoons olive oil

1 yellow onion, roughly chopped

3 celery stalks, roughly chopped

2 garlic cloves, roughly chopped

7 flat-leaf parsley sprigs, plus additional chopped parsley for garnish

1 (3-pound) bone-in pork butt

¼ teaspoon salt

¼ teaspoon ground black pepper

1 pound dried navy beans

4 cups reduced-sodium chicken broth

4 cups water

12 ounces tomato sauce

1 pound ditalini pasta

4 ounces Pecorino Romano cheese, grated

1. Set a pressure cooker to the sauté function and heat the olive oil. Add the onion, celery, garlic, and parsley and sauté until softened.

2. Season the pork butt all over with the salt and pepper and add to the pot, along with the navy beans, chicken broth, water, and tomato sauce. Cover and cook at high pressure for 55 minutes.

3. When the soup is nearly done, bring a large pot of water to a boil and cook the pasta for 2 minutes less than the package instructions. Drain.

4. When the soup is done, transfer the pork butt to a plate and stir the pasta into the pot. Pull the pork with two forks until it's shredded, then return it to the pot and stir well. Discard the bone.

5. Once the pasta is al dente, ladle the soup into bowls and top with the grated cheese and chopped parsley.

Bun Rieu

Vietnamese Pork and Crab Meatball Soup

Foo

The unctuous crab and pork meatballs in this soup are flavorful and irresistibly funky, balanced out by the delicate pineapple, tomato, and chicken-flavored stock. Combined with delicate rice noodles and garnished with fresh herbs, it's a noodle soup everyone will enjoy. **Serves 6**

---

1 tablespoon vegetable oil

1 Vidalia onion, finely chopped

8 ounces blue crabmeat, finely chopped

2 tablespoons crab paste with soybean oil

2 tablespoons fermented shrimp paste, divided

1 (6-ounce) can tomato paste

1 pound shrimp, peeled, deveined, and finely chopped

Salt and ground black pepper to taste

1 pound ground pork

2 large eggs, lightly beaten

1 bunch scallions, finely chopped

5 quarts chicken broth

8 cups water

3 tablespoons Chinese rock sugar (see note on page 54)

2 tablespoons fish sauce

1 pound tomatoes, quartered

1 pineapple, peeled, cored, and cut into chunks

1 pound vermicelli noodles, cooked according to package instructions

8 ounces bean sprouts

½ bunch mint, leaves picked

½ bunch perilla, leaves picked (or more mint)

1 lemon, sliced

---

1. Heat the oil in a large skillet over medium heat. Add the onion, crabmeat, crab paste, 1 tablespoon of the fermented shrimp paste, the tomato paste, shrimp, salt, and pepper and sauté for 10 minutes.

2. Transfer the crabmeat mixture to a bowl and let cool slightly. Add the ground pork, eggs, and scallions and mix well. Form the mixture into meatballs about 2 inches in diameter.

3. In a large pot, combine the chicken broth and water. Bring to a steady boil, then add the rock sugar, fish sauce, remaining 1 tablespoon shrimp paste, and tomatoes. Slowly add the pork and crab meatballs. Bring back to a steady boil for 15 minutes, then add the pineapple.

4. Divide the noodles into soup bowls and ladle the soup over the noodles. Garnish with the bean sprouts, herbs, and lemon slices.

Mrs. Nguyen's Pho

Foo

This deep beef-flavored soup is Vietnam's national dish, served throughout the country for breakfast, lunch, and dinner. Traditionally, the broth can take days to make to capture the depth of flavor; in this recipe, I use pho soup base and a seasoning packet to get all that flavor in much less time. The noodles and fresh herbs complement the complexities of the broth. **Serves 6**

Pickled onions

¼ cup white vinegar

¼ cup rice vinegar

½ cup water

¼ cup sugar

½ teaspoon kosher salt

1 red onion, thinly sliced

Pho

1 bunch scallions

3 shallots

2 large knobs ginger

1 beef rib

3 beef oxtails

5 quarts water

1 (2.64-ounce) packet pho seasoning
(star anise, cinnamon, cardamom,
coriander seeds)

3 tablespoons Chinese rock sugar (see
note on page 54)

2 tablespoons pho soup base

1 tablespoon chicken bouillon powder

2 tablespoons salt, plus more to taste

1 (8-ounce) package pho noodles

2 tablespoons vegetable oil, optional

1 boneless ribeye steak

Ground black pepper to taste

2 tablespoons BBQ dry rub

1 lime, cut in half

8 ounces bean sprouts

1 bunch cilantro, leaves picked

1 bunch Thai basil, leaves picked

2 jalapeños, thinly sliced

1. To make the pickled onions, combine the white vinegar, rice vinegar, water, sugar, and salt in a bowl and stir until the sugar and salt dissolve. Add the red onion and stir. Cover and refrigerate for 30 minutes.

2. Char the scallions, shallots, and ginger over a stovetop flame (or on a grill) until blackened and aromatic. Set aside.

3. Fill a large pot with water and bring to a rolling boil. Add the beef rib and oxtails and boil for 15 minutes. Drain and rinse the meat with cold water.

4. Pour the water into a pressure cooker. Add the beef rib, oxtails, scallions, shallots, ginger, pho seasoning, rock sugar, soup base, chicken bouillon, and salt. Select the "stew" mode and set for 1 hour.

5. Meanwhile, place the dry pho noodles in a large bowl, cover with hot water, and let soak for 20 minutes. Drain the noodles and rinse under cold water, then divide into soup bowls.

6. Preheat the grill to medium heat, or heat the vegetable oil in a skillet over medium heat. Rub the ribeye steak all over with salt, pepper, and BBQ dry rub. Grill or sear the steak for 3 minutes on each side. Transfer the steak to a cutting board and let it rest for 5 minutes, then slice against the grain. Squeeze the lime all over the steak.

7. When the pressure cooker is finished, ladle the broth over the noodles. Separate the meat from the rib and oxtails and add it to the noodles and broth. Fan the sliced ribeye over the soup and garnish with the bean sprouts, herbs, pickled red onions, and 3 thin slices of jalapeño.

Chloe's Halftime: Vietnamese Beef Stew

with Cabbage Salad

This aromatic, sweet, spicy, robust, and savory Vietnamese beef stew, topped with a slice of toasted baguette, is a perfect meal to keep you cozy and feed your soul when you're enjoying Sunday football in the fall or sheltering from the cold. It's one of the few dishes Chloe, our seven-year-old, will happily finish—and she'll even lick the bowl. Enjoy the stew alongside a Japanese-inspired cabbage salad with soy sauce vinaigrette. **Serves 6**

Beef stew

¼ cup Vietnamese bò kho seasoning (see note)

2 lemongrass stalks, minced

5 garlic cloves, minced

2 shallots, minced

Salt and ground black pepper to taste

1½ pounds beef roast, cut into 2-inch cubes

2 tablespoons vegetable oil

2 tablespoons Chinese rock sugar (see note)

1 (12-ounce) can coconut water

2 (14.5-ounce) cans beef broth

3 carrots, peeled and cut into 1-inch pieces

1 small potato, peeled and cut into 1-inch cubes

1 baguette

1 bunch Thai basil leaves, for garnish

Cabbage salad

1 small head green cabbage, cored

2 tablespoons rice vinegar

2 tablespoons Maggi seasoning, soy sauce, or Worcestershire sauce

1 tablespoon toasted sesame oil

1 tablespoon sugar

Juice of 1 lime wedge

Toasted sesame seeds

---

1. In a large bowl, combine the bò kho seasoning, lemongrass, garlic, shallots, salt, and pepper. Add the beef and toss to coat the meat with the mixture.

2. Heat the vegetable oil in a cast iron skillet over medium-high heat. Sear the seasoned meat but do not cook the meat all the way through. Transfer the seared meat to a pressure cooker.

3. Add the rock sugar, coconut water, beef broth, carrots, and potato. Select "stew" mode on the pressure cooker and set for 30 minutes.

4. Meanwhile, preheat the oven to 350 degrees F.

5. To make the cabbage salad, thinly shred the cabbage using a mandoline or knife. In a medium bowl, whisk together the vinegar, Maggi seasoning, sesame oil, sugar, and lime juice. Add the shredded cabbage and toss to coat. Top with the sesame seeds.

(recipe continues)

6. Place the baguette on a baking sheet and toast in the oven for 15 minutes. Remove and slice.

7. When the pressure cooker completes the cooking cycle, ladle the stew into soup bowls and garnish with Thai basil and additional black pepper. Serve with baguette slices.

Note: This recipe calls for a couple of traditional East Asian ingredients that may be new to you. Bò kho seasoning, or Vietnamese beef stew seasoning, is a blend of spices including paprika, star anise, garlic, chile, ginger, clove, and sometimes annatto. If you can't find it at your grocery store, look online, or you can try this recipe with Chinese five-spice powder instead. Chinese rock sugar, also called Chinese sugar or Chinese sugar crystal, consists of lumps of white sugar crystals that are clear or yellowish in color and less sweet than regular white sugar. White sugar will work as a substitute.

Moqueca and Pão de Queijo

Robin

Brazilian Seafood Stew and Cheese Bread

I love my family, so when my four children grew up and I became an empty nester, I knew it was time for an adventure. Tomio, my oldest, was studying in Brazil, so I up and moved to be near him. I spoke no Portuguese and I relied on Tomio to help me until I learned the new language. In Brazil, I shared my family's recipes with my new Brazilian friends, and they taught me their own family favorites in return. Moqueca infuses so many of the flavors characteristic to Brazil. This chowder, made with a massive selection of regional seafood, is unlike any I've ever had. Don't skip the pão de queijo to serve alongside it! It is rich in both flavor and history. Made with the type of flour available to the earliest people of Brazil, this cheese bread is treasured by all. **Serves 6**

Pão de queijo

1 large egg

½ cup olive oil

1 cup whole milk

1 cup grated Pecorino Romano cheese

¼ cup chopped fresh chives

2 cups tapioca flour

2 tablespoons potato starch

½ teaspoon salt

Moqueca

Salt to taste

2 large potatoes, peeled and chopped

1 pound cod or other firm white fish, cut into bite-size pieces

8 ounces sea scallops, cut into bite-size pieces

Juice of 2 limes, divided

4 garlic cloves, minced

1 pound large shrimp, peeled with tails left on, deveined, and cleaned

2 tablespoons olive oil

2 tablespoons dendê oil, palm oil, or coconut oil, divided (see note)

1 teaspoon paprika (optional, see note)

1 large onion, chopped

3 bell peppers (preferably different colors), seeded and chopped

1 large bunch cilantro, stems finely chopped, leaves left whole, divided

2 jalapeños, finely chopped

2 large tomatoes, finely chopped

1 teaspoon smoked paprika

1 cup canned hearts of palm, drained and chopped

1 cup bottled clam juice

1 cup canned full-fat coconut milk

Red pepper flakes to taste

---

1. Preheat the oven to 400 degrees F. Line a muffin tin with paper liners.

2. In a large bowl, whisk together the egg, oil, and milk. Stir in the cheese and chives.

3. In a separate bowl, whisk together the tapioca flour, potato starch, and salt. Slowly add the dry ingredients to the wet ingredients. Mix well until the dough comes together. If it is sticky, add a little more tapioca flour; if is dry, add a little more milk.

(recipe continues)

4. With an ice cream scoop, scoop balls of dough into the lined muffin cups. Bake for 15–20 minutes, until the tops begin to turn golden and crack.

5. While the pão de queijo is in the oven, bring a medium pot of salted water to a boil. Add the potatoes and cook until tender, about 7 minutes. Drain, rinse, and set aside.

6. Meanwhile, put the cod and scallops in a large bowl. Add the juice of 1 lime, the garlic, and salt, toss to coat, and set aside.

7. In a separate bowl, toss the shrimp with the olive oil and juice of the remaining lime and set aside.

8. Heat 1½ tablespoons of the dendê oil (or coconut oil with 1 teaspoon paprika; see note) in a large pot over medium heat. Add the onion, bell peppers, cilantro stems, and jalapeños and cook, stirring, for 2 minutes. Add the tomatoes and paprika and cook, stirring, for 1 minute more. Gently fold in the cod, scallops, potatoes, hearts of palm, clam juice, and coconut milk. Bring to a boil, then reduce the heat, cover, and simmer for 10 minutes. Add red pepper flakes as desired. Turn off the heat and uncover the pot.

9. In a saucepan, heat the remaining ½ tablespoon dendê oil (or coconut oil) over medium heat. Add the shrimp, a few red pepper flakes, and salt and quickly sear the shrimp just until they turn bright orange, about 2 minutes. Transfer the shrimp to a plate and reserve the oil in the pan for drizzling on the chowder before serving.

10. Ladle the chowder into rustic crock-type bowls. Place several shrimp in the center of the bowl, garnish with the cilantro leaves, and drizzle the shrimp cooking oil across the top of each bowl. Serve the pão de queijo alongside.

Note: If you can't find dendê oil or palm oil, coconut oil is the closest substitution. Add the optional paprika to retain the traditional color.

Cioppino

Nikki

My family is from Calabria, Italy, but I grew up in the Pacific Northwest—two places where fresh seafood is in abundance and easily accessible. Every year, we take a trip to the Oregon coast to visit a restaurant that makes a stellar cioppino, the classic Italian American fish stew. Cioppino broth includes tomatoes, garlic, onions, and wine (I like to use Elk Cove Pinot Gris, a local Oregon white wine). I usually opt for whatever fresh local seafood I find for this dish, and I encourage you to seek out local seafood for your cioppino if you can. **Serves 4**

(recipe continues)

4 tablespoons olive oil, divided

1 medium yellow onion, diced

4 garlic cloves, sliced

2 teaspoons dried parsley

1 tablespoon dried oregano

1 tablespoon dried Italian seasoning

1 teaspoon sea salt, plus more to taste

Ground black pepper to taste

½ teaspoon red pepper flakes

2 (28-ounce) cans diced San Marzano tomatoes

2 cups dry white wine

1 pound cod fillets, cut into pieces

1 pound littleneck clams

8 ounces mussels, cleaned and debearded

8 ounces bay scallops

8 ounces large shrimp, peeled and deveined

1 baguette, cut into ½-inch slices

1 bunch flat-leaf parsley, leaves picked

1 bunch basil, leaves picked

½ cup grated Parmesan cheese

1 lemon, cut into wedges

1. In a large pot, heat 2 tablespoons of the olive oil over medium heat. Add the onion and sauté for 1–2 minutes. Add the garlic, dried parsley, oregano, Italian seasoning, salt, black pepper, and red pepper flakes and continue to sauté until a paste forms. Add the tomatoes with their juices and the wine and mix well.

2. Add the cod, clams, mussels, and scallops, cover the pot, and cook for 10 minutes.

3. Add the shrimp, cover again, and cook for 5 more minutes. You'll know it's done when the shrimp are opaque and pink and the clams and mussels have opened. Remove and discard any unopened clams or mussels.

4. Turn on the oven broiler. Place the baguette slices on a rimmed baking sheet and brush with the remaining 2 tablespoons olive oil. Broil for about 2 minutes, or until slightly toasted.

5. Ladle the cioppino into shallow pasta dishes and garnish with the fresh parsley and basil and grated Parmesan cheese. Serve with lemon wedges for squeezing and crostini pieces to sop up the broth.

Beet, Fig, and Pine Nut Salad in Endive

Robin

Sweet, nutty, and slightly bitter, this salad is a dish of great balance. A chopped salad of roasted beets, figs, pine nuts, and pancetta is served inside endive leaves with a dollop of yogurt and a sprinkle of microgreens for a truly elegant presentation. I made this salad alongside my Fish in a Fig Leaf (page 145) in the finale of *The Great American Recipe* because I wanted to showcase the fig in a variety of ways as it represents my life: sweet, nutty, and sometimes bitter. It felt like everything in my life had brought me to that moment. **Serves: 4**

Salad

2 medium red beets

2 medium gold beets

1 garlic head (see note)

5 ounces pancetta, diced

4 Mission figs, pitted and halved

¼ cup pine nuts

2 purple endive

2 green endive

1 bunch spring onions, finely chopped

½ cup plain Greek-style yogurt

1 bunch microgreens

Dressing

2 tablespoons olive oil

2 tablespoons maple syrup

1 tablespoon fresh lemon juice

1 tablespoon fig balsamic vinegar

1 teaspoon Dijon mustard

Salt to taste

Cayenne pepper to taste

1. Preheat the oven to 400 degrees F.

2. Wrap the beets and garlic head in parchment paper and then in aluminum foil and place in a small baking pan. Roast for about 20 minutes, until tender but not mushy. Let cool, then peel the beets and chop confetti size, keeping the red separate from the gold. Reserve 3 roasted garlic cloves for the dressing and save the rest for another use.

3. Meanwhile, crisp the pancetta in a small skillet over medium heat. Using a slotted spoon, transfer the pancetta to a plate. In the same skillet, caramelize the halved figs quickly, then transfer to the plate. Toast the pine nuts in the same pan and transfer to the plate. When the figs are cool enough to handle, cut into confetti.

4. Pick apart the endive leaves, placing 1 green and 1 purple leaf on each plate.

5. In a large bowl, combine all the dressing ingredients. Squeeze the reserved 3 roasted garlic cloves out of their skins and into the bowl and whisk well to combine. Add the beets, pancetta, figs, pine nuts, and spring onions and gently mix the salad ingredients with the dressing. Arrange spoonfuls in each endive leaf, then top with a tiny dollop of yogurt and a bit of microgreens.

Note: You will have some roasted garlic cloves left over. On *The Great American Recipe*, I served this salad alongside Fish in a Fig Leaf (page 145). If you're serving those dishes together, reserve the pancetta drippings and 2 roasted garlic cloves from this recipe to make the fig sauce. ***This dish is pictured on page 144.***

Spring Pea Salad with Preserved Lemon and Celery Seed Vinaigrette

Tiffany

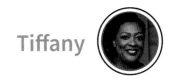

I call my style Southern cooking but you'll often hear it described as "modern Southern" because I like to take traditional ingredients and recipes and present them in a fresh new way. This salad is a great example: it's snap peas, snow peas, or fava beans (or a combination), radishes, and herbs tossed in a preserved lemon vinaigrette and served with candied bacon. You'll have extra dressing left over, but I bet you'll find lots of ways to use it up—it's that good. **Serves 4**

Vinaigrette

2½ cups olive oil

1 cup fresh lemon juice

1 preserved lemon, chopped, including rind and flesh

2 garlic cloves, chopped

1 tablespoon celery seed, toasted and ground

1 tablespoon salt

1 teaspoon sugar

Salad

12 ounces snap peas, snow peas, and/or fava beans

4 ounces radishes, thinly sliced

Salt and ground black pepper to taste

8 basil leaves, torn

8 mint leaves, torn

¼ cup roughly chopped fresh dill

8 ounces burrata cheese

Frisée lettuce, for garnish

½ cup finely chopped candied bacon

Olive oil, for drizzling

1. To make the vinaigrette, in a medium bowl, whisk together all the ingredients; set aside.

2. Fill a large pot with water and bring to a boil. Fill a large bowl with water and ice cubes. Add the peas to the boiling water and blanch for 1 minute. Use a slotted spoon to transfer the peas to the ice bath. Once cool, drain well and pat dry.

3. In a large bowl, combine the blanched peas, radishes, and ¼ cup of the vinaigrette. Season with salt and pepper. Add the basil, mint, and dill and toss again. Add more dressing if desired. (Leftover dressing can be stored in an airtight container in the refrigerator for up to two weeks.)

4. Arrange the salad in a ring on a serving plate. Lay the burrata in the center. Garnish with a few strands of frisée. Top with the candied bacon, drizzle with olive oil, and serve.

Grilled Calamari Mango Salad

Foo

My family is from a coastal town in Vietnam where seafood is abundant, and we have this dish every year for Christmas. The seasoned char-grilled calamari provide a sweet and spicy complement to the sweet and sour mango slices. The herbs add a fresh flavorful element that is a key factor to the balance of this dish. It's all finished with a sweet and salty fish sauce dressing to provide an umami flavor that harmoniously marries the salad together. **Serves 6**

Calamari

1 tablespoon fish sauce

1 tablespoon chili paste

1 tablespoon sugar

1 teaspoon chili sauce

4 garlic cloves, minced

2 fresh Thai chile peppers, minced

Salt and ground black pepper to taste

3 pounds calamari

Mango salad

3 tablespoons fish sauce

1 tablespoon white vinegar

1 tablespoon sugar

2 teaspoons chili paste

Juice of 1 lime wedge

1 cup warm water

5 firm green or orange mangos, peeled, pitted, and cut into thin strips

1 tablespoon garlic salt

1 bunch Thai basil, leaves picked and coarsely chopped

1 bunch mint, leaves picked and coarsely chopped

1 bunch cilantro, leaves picked and coarsely chopped

6 fresh Thai chile peppers, finely chopped

1 (3.5-ounce) package sesame rice crackers

3 tablespoons fried shallots

¼ cup roasted unsalted Virginia peanuts, ground in a mortar and pestle to a coarse consistency

1. In a large bowl, whisk together the fish sauce, chili paste, sugar, chili sauce, garlic, Thai chiles, and salt and pepper. Add the calamari and toss to coat. Cover and marinate in the refrigerator for 30 minutes.

2. Meanwhile, to make the salad, in a small bowl, whisk together the fish sauce, vinegar, sugar, chili paste, lime juice, and water. Stir to dissolve and blend all the ingredients. Add the mango strips, garlic salt, chopped herbs, and chile peppers and toss to coat. Set aside.

3. Preheat a grill. Grill the calamari, then cut into thin strips and toss with the mango salad.

4. Place the rice crackers on a microwave- safe plate and microwave on high for 2 minutes, or until the crackers bubble and turn completely white.

5. Transfer the salad to a serving platter and garnish with the fried shallots and peanuts. Serve the crackers on the side.

Steak Salad

This ribeye steak salad is rich and unctuous thanks to a marinade made from oyster sauce and black bean sauce. The salty and savory components of the seared steak complement the multilayered salad underneath, with roasted carrots and Brussels sprouts, blanched green beans, and fresh herbs that add depth to the dish. Like me, this salad might seem "unassuming," but it is full of depth and many layers. **Serves 6**

Steak

2 tablespoons oyster sauce

2 tablespoons black bean sauce

1 shallot, minced

3 garlic cloves, minced

Salt and ground black pepper

2 boneless ribeye steaks

1 lime

Salad

6 carrots, peeled and cut into 1-inch pieces

6 Brussels sprouts, cut in half

3 tablespoons olive oil, divided

1 teaspoon dried oregano

Salt and ground black pepper to taste

12 green beans

2 tablespoons white vinegar

1 teaspoon balsamic vinegar

1 tablespoon Dijon mustard

Juice of 1 lime wedge

1 tablespoon sugar

1 tablespoon minced shallot

6 hard-boiled quail eggs, cut in half

1 cucumber, sliced

1 bunch mint, leaves picked and chopped

1 bunch dill, chopped

1 head romaine lettuce, leaves chopped

---

1. Preheat the oven to 350 degrees F.

2. In a small bowl, mix the oyster sauce, black bean sauce, shallot, garlic, and salt and pepper. Spread the marinade on the steaks and let sit at room temperature for 30 minutes.

3. Meanwhile, put the carrots and Brussels sprouts on a rimmed baking sheet. Drizzle with 1 tablespoon of the olive oil and season with the oregano, salt, and pepper. Spread out the carrots and Brussels sprouts and roast for 30 minutes.

4. While the vegetables are roasting, bring a small pot of water to a boil and blanch the green beans; drain.

5. In a large bowl, whisk together the remaining 2 tablespoons olive oil, the white vinegar, balsamic vinegar, mustard, lime juice, sugar, shallot, salt, and pepper. Add the roasted carrots and Brussels sprouts, blanched green beans, quail eggs, cucumber, mint, dill, and romaine lettuce and set aside.

6. Preheat a grill over high heat.

7. Grill the steaks for 15–20 minutes on each side for medium-rare, or to the desired doneness. Let the steaks rest for 10 minutes. Slice the steaks against the grain, arrange over the salad, and serve.

Handhelds

Spam Banh Mi with BBQ Shrimp Chips

Foo

I like to share banh mi with my friends and family at picnics and other outings. This comfort food has all the elements you want in a sandwich. The saltiness from the canned meat complements the acidic pickled daikon and red onions, while the cilantro and cucumber provide a fresh element to counter the richness of the canned meat and mayo. The combined ingredients nestled in a seasoned warm baguette are enhanced by a side of crunchy fried BBQ-flavored shrimp chips, a classic Southeast Asian snack. I inherited the recipe from my mom and have elevated it with my own homemade sauce. **Serves 6**

Pickled vegetables

1 cup hot water

½ cup white vinegar

½ cup rice vinegar

½ cup white sugar

1 teaspoon kosher salt

1 small daikon, grated

2 carrots, peeled and grated

1 small red onion, thinly sliced

Spread

3 tablespoons ranch dressing

3 tablespoons mayonnaise

1 kosher dill pickle, chopped

Banh mi

2 baguettes

2 tablespoons vegetable oil

1 (12-ounce) can Spam, thinly sliced

3 tablespoons Maggi seasoning or soy sauce

3 tablespoons European butter, such as Plugra

3 tablespoons sriracha

Ground black pepper to taste

3 jalapeños, sliced

2 bunches cilantro

1 cucumber, sliced

BBQ shrimp chips

½ cup brown sugar

¼ cup garlic powder

3 tablespoons smoked paprika

3 tablespoons cayenne pepper

2 tablespoons sea salt

Vegetable oil, for deep frying

1 (6-ounce) bag shrimp chips

1. First, make the pickled vegetables. Combine the water, white vinegar, rice vinegar, white sugar, and salt in a bowl and stir until the salt and sugar dissolve. Add the daikon, carrots, and red onion and stir. Cover and refrigerate for 30 minutes.

2. In a small bowl, whisk together the ranch, mayo, and chopped pickle to create a spread. Cover and refrigerate until ready to serve.

3. Preheat the oven to 300 degrees F. Put the baguettes on a rimmed baking sheet and bake for 10 minutes.

(recipe continues)

4. Meanwhile, heat the vegetable oil in a skillet over medium-high heat, then fry the Spam until golden and crispy.

5. Split the baguettes open lengthwise and spread with the Maggi seasoning, butter, ranch-mayo spread, and sriracha. Add the black pepper, jalapeño slices, cilantro, cucumber, and pickled vegetables. Add the Spam and tie butcher's twine in a bow to help loosely close the sandwiches.

6. To make the shrimp chips, combine the brown sugar, garlic powder, smoked paprika, cayenne pepper, and sea salt in a large bowl and mix.

7. Pour the oil into a deep fryer or large, heavy-bottomed pot and heat to 350 degrees F. Add the shrimp chips and fry until the chips turn fluffy and crispy, about 2 minutes.

8. Transfer the hot cooked shrimp chips to the bowl with the BBQ seasonings and toss well to coat.

9. Cut the banh mi sandwiches into thirds and serve with the shrimp chips.

Tortas de Milanesa

Silvia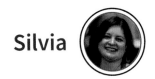

Chicken Cutlet Sandwiches with Mexican-Style Limeade

A torta is a Mexican sandwich made with either a traditional bolillo roll (which has a hardier, crispy exterior) or a telera roll (which has a flatter shape and softer exterior). This torta features milanesa de pollo, which is a well-seasoned, succulent, crunchy, breaded chicken cutlet. The secret is to season at every step, from the milk to the flour to the bread crumbs. Top with tomatoes, cheese, avocado, lettuce, cilantro, mayo, and, most importantly, pickled jalapeños. **Serves 4**

Milanesas

4 (3- to 4-ounce) chicken cutlets

1 cup milk

3 teaspoons salt, divided

1½ teaspoons freshly ground black pepper, divided

2 cups all-purpose flour

2 teaspoons onion powder, divided

2 teaspoons garlic powder, divided

2 teaspoons paprika, divided

2 large eggs

2 cups bread crumbs

½–1 cup vegetable oil

Tortas

4 bolillo or telera rolls, approximately 7 inches long

¼ cup mayonnaise

1 (12-ounce) can pickled sliced jalapeños, drained, with 2 tablespoons vinegar reserved

1 large ripe avocado

½ cup mayonnaise with lime juice (or ½ cup plain mayonnaise mixed with fresh lime juice to taste)

4 iceberg lettuce leaves

8 slices Oaxaca cheese

2 tomatoes, sliced

Cilantro sprigs, for garnish

---

1. Place a chicken cutlet between two sheets of plastic wrap and pound with a meat tenderizer to an even ¼-inch thickness. Repeat with all the cutlets.

2. In a large bowl, whisk together the milk, 1 teaspoon salt, and ½ teaspoon pepper. Add the cutlets, cover, and let soak for 10–15 minutes.

3. Set up three shallow bowls for coating the chicken. In the first bowl, mix the flour, 1 teaspoon of the onion powder, 1 teaspoon of the garlic powder, 1 teaspoon of the paprika, 1 teaspoon of the salt, and ½ teaspoon of the pepper. In the second bowl, beat the eggs. In the third bowl, mix the bread crumbs with the remaining 1 teaspoon onion powder, remaining 1 teaspoon garlic powder, remaining 1 teaspoon paprika, remaining 1 teaspoon salt, and remaining ½ teaspoon black pepper.

4. Drain the chicken cutlets and pat them dry with paper towels. Dredge one chicken cutlet through the flour, then shake off any excess. Cover both sides with the egg, and finally place the chicken

(recipe continues)

in the bread crumbs, pressing both sides to make sure it's completely covered. Transfer to a plate. Repeat until all the cutlets are breaded. Line a large plate with paper towels.

5. In a nonstick skillet, heat ½ cup of the oil over medium-high heat. Pan-fry two cutlets at a time for 3–4 minutes per side. Transfer to the paper towels. Repeat to fry all the chicken. If needed, wipe out the skillet and add more oil between batches to get rid of any burned pieces of breading.

6. Preheat the oven to 350 degrees F.

7. Place the rolls on a rimmed baking sheet and warm them up in the oven for 5–7 minutes. Slice them in half.

8. Meanwhile, in a small bowl, whisk together the plain mayonnaise and 1 tablespoon of the reserved vinegar from the pickled jalapeños. If the spicy mayo is too thick, add more vinegar, a teaspoon at a time, to get your desired consistency.

9. When ready to assemble the tortas, peel, pit, and slice the avocado. Spread 1 tablespoon lime mayo on the bottom half of each roll. Add a lettuce leaf, then 2 slices of cheese, a chicken cutlet, some tomato slices, pickled jalapeños, avocado, and finally a cilantro sprig. Top with some of the spicy mayo and close the sandwich with the top half of the roll.

Mexican-Style Limeade

8–10 cups water

1 cup sugar

4 large thin-skinned limes, divided
(2 cut in half, 2 for garnishing)

Ice cubes

1. Combine 2 cups of the water and the sugar in a blender and blend for 15 seconds, or until the sugar is dissolved. Add the 2 halved limes and blend for 4–5 seconds. Strain the mixture into a pitcher, add another 6–8 cups water, and mix well. Taste and add more sugar if needed. Add lots of ice and garnish with lime slices.

Salsiccia, Rabe, and Provolone Panini

Dan

with Homemade Potato Chips

This my go-to handheld dish. I always have sausage and peppers in the fridge and a loaf of bread in the pantry, and I grow my own broccoli rabe—but you don't need to be a gardener to enjoy this classic flavor combination. This sandwich is substantial enough to fill you up, but it's not messy, so it travels easily (and can be eaten standing up!). **Serves 6**

6 links hot Italian sausage

½ cup water

8 tablespoons olive oil, divided

2 heads broccoli rabe, stems removed

2 tablespoons plus ¼ teaspoon kosher salt, divided

8 garlic cloves, thinly sliced

½ teaspoon red pepper flakes

2 red bell peppers

¼ teaspoon ground black pepper

6 hard Italian rolls, split open

8 ounces Provolone cheese, sliced

4 ounces Pecorino Romano cheese, grated

Fried potato chips

Vegetable oil, for deep frying

2 Idaho potatoes, thinly sliced on a mandoline

¼ teaspoon kosher salt

1. In a large skillet, combine the sausages, water, and 2 tablespoons of the olive oil. Cook over medium heat until the water has evaporated and the sausages are browned, 10–15 minutes. Set aside.

2. Bring a large pot of water to a boil. Fill a large bowl with cold water and ice cubes. Add the broccoli rabe to the boiling water along with 2 tablespoons of the kosher salt. Cook for 4 minutes, then transfer to the ice bath.

3. Meanwhile, in another skillet, heat another 4 tablespoons olive oil over low heat. Add the garlic and red pepper flakes and cook just until the garlic is slightly browned.

4. Drain the broccoli rabe, add it to the skillet with the garlic, and cook until tender and all the remaining water has evaporated. Set aside while you make the potato chips.

5. Pour the vegetable oil into a deep fryer or large, heavy-bottomed pot and heat to 350 degrees F. Line a rimmed baking sheet with paper towels.

6. Add the sliced potatoes to the hot oil and cook until crispy. Using a slotted spoon or spider, transfer the potato chips to the paper towels. Sprinkle with the salt.

7. Char the bell peppers over the open flame of a gas stove until all the skin is black. Place the peppers in a bowl, cover with plastic wrap, and let sit until the peppers have completely cooled. Remove the skins, cut in half, and remove the seeds. Cut the peppers into thin strips and put them back in the bowl. Add the remaining 2 tablespoons olive oil, remaining ¼ teaspoon kosher salt, and the black pepper. Toss well.

8. On each roll, place one sausage, then a few slices of Provolone, then some of the rabe and roasted bell pepper strips. Top with the grated Pecorino Romano. Serve the chips on the side.

Date Macadamia Chicken Salad Sandwiches

Silvia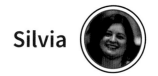

The first time I tried a version of this chicken salad, introduced to me by my husband's cousin Cheryl, I fell in love with the sweet and savory flavors and the crunchy, nutty texture. I asked for the recipe immediately. I added my own twist, incorporating celery for even more crunch and freshness, as well as pickled jalapeños for a kick of spice and acidity. Dates, bacon, celery, and macadamia nuts elevate classic chicken salad to new sweet and savory heights. Be sure to serve on toasted bread. **Serves 6**

1½ pounds boneless, skinless chicken breasts

2 rosemary sprigs

4 garlic cloves, peeled

1½ teaspoons salt

8 bacon slices

6 small ciabatta rolls

10 medium dates, pitted and finely chopped

½ cup chopped macadamia nuts, finely chopped

2 celery stalks, finely chopped

6 scallions, finely chopped

1 cup mayonnaise

1 head butterhead lettuce

1 (12-ounce) can pickled jalapeños, drained

---

1. Preheat the oven to 400 degrees F. Line a rimmed baking sheet with aluminum foil.

2. Put the chicken, rosemary, garlic, and salt in a large pot. Cover with water and bring to a boil. Cover the pot, reduce the heat to medium-high, and cook until the chicken is tender, 25–30 minutes. Transfer the chicken to a plate to cool.

3. Meanwhile, spread out the bacon on the lined baking sheet and bake, turning once, until cooked through and crispy, about 4 minutes per side. Transfer the bacon to paper towels, then chop. Turn down the oven temperature to 350 degrees F.

4. Warm up the ciabatta rolls in the oven for 5–8 min.

5. When the chicken is cool enough to handle, shred the meat and put it in a large bowl. Add the bacon, dates, macadamia nuts, celery, scallions, and mayonnaise. Mix well and taste for salt; add more if needed.

6. Cut the rolls in half. Place a layer of lettuce on the bottom half, add a few tablespoons of the chicken salad, and top with pickled jalapeños.

Scallop BLTs
Seared Scallops with Stewed Tomatoes, Grilled Romaine, and Bacon Vinaigrette

Graham

I love to say that there is no right or wrong when it comes to cooking—everything is open to your interpretation. As long as you cook with love, and with fresh ingredients that are local and in season, then you can pretty much go in whatever direction you want. This dish is a play on the classic BLT. Bacon, lettuce, and tomatoes are three food besties that love to hang out on the plate. With the addition of scallops, the dish is next-level! Feel free to substitute any type of fish or even chicken, and remember you can swap the bacon, lettuce, and tomato components with any number of things (as long as you use those ingredients, or else it wouldn't be a BLT). Bon appétit! **Serves 2**

---

6 Roma tomatoes, sliced and seeded

1 medium onion, sliced

½ bunch fresh basil leaves

½ cup plus 3 tablespoons olive oil, divided

1 shallot, sliced

4 slices bacon, chopped

¼ cup balsamic vinegar

8 large sea scallops

Kosher salt

Black pepper

1 lemon

2 Romaine hearts

2 tablespoons butter

2 thick slices brioche

¼ cup mayonnaise or aioli

---

1. Put the tomatoes in a small sauté pan over low heat. Add the sliced onion and basil and cover with ½ cup of the olive oil. Simmer on low heat for 15 minutes, then turn the heat off.

2. In another sauté pan, cook the shallot, stirring occasionally, for 1 to 2 minutes until slightly soft. Add the bacon and render till crispy. Remove some of the drippings and add the balsamic vinegar; remove from heat.

3. Season the scallops with salt and pepper. Heat 2 tablespoons of the olive oil in another sauté pan over medium heat. Sear the scallops for 2 minutes, then flip and cook for 1 to 2 minutes more, until golden brown on both sides. Remove to a plate, drizzle with juice from the lemon, and tent with foil if needed to keep warm until you're ready to serve.

4. Toss the romaine hearts in 1 tablespoon of the olive oil (or enough to coat). Heat a grill pan over medium-high heat and grill the romaine for 1 to 2 minutes, or until slightly charred and wilted. Give the romaine hearts a rough chop.

5. Melt the butter in another pan over medium-high heat. Sauté the brioche till warm and toasted.

6. Strain the oil from the tomato and onion mixture. Place each slice of brioche on a serving plate. Top with the tomatoes, romaine, and scallops, and then spoon some of the bacon vinaigrette on top. Garnish with aioli.

L'Italiano Burger

Dan

For me, there's nothing more American than a good old-fashioned burger. I serve these burgers every year in June to celebrate Gaspee Days, a New England holiday commemorating one of the first uprisings leading to the Revolutionary War. This is a big holiday in my hometown because the event occurred in Rhode Island, where I am from. This burger is a staple at this celebration. Of course, the all-American burger gets some great additions inspired by my Italian roots: it's topped with melty mozzarella, crispy prosciutto, and a peppery arugula insalata. **Serves 6**

Calabrian chile oil

3 tablespoons olive oil

10 dried Calabrian chiles, minced

Crispy prosciutto

1 tablespoon olive oil

12 slices prosciutto di Parma

Italian ketchup

20 dried Calabrian chiles, stemmed

1½ pounds plum tomatoes

1 large shallot, peeled

2 garlic cloves, peeled

¾ teaspoon kosher salt

½ teaspoon sugar

1 tablespoon vegetable oil

Burgers

3 tablespoons salted butter

1½ pounds ground chuck

12 ounces ground short ribs

12 ounces ground tri-tip

2 pounds whole-milk, low-moisture mozzarella cheese, cut into 6 equal pieces

6 potato rolls, cut in half and toasted or grilled

Arugula insalata

2 tablespoons fresh lemon juice

½ teaspoon kosher salt

¼ teaspoon ground black pepper

1½ cups packed baby arugula

---

1. First, make the Calabrian chile oil, which will be used in the arugula insalata. Heat the olive oil in a small skillet over medium-low heat. Add the Calabrian chiles and cook, stirring occasionally, for 40 minutes. Strain, reserving the oil and the chiles separately. Set aside.

2. Next, make the crispy prosciutto. Heat the olive oil in a large skillet over medium heat. Add 6 slices of prosciutto and cook until crispy, then transfer to paper towels. Repeat to cook the other 6 slices. Set aside.

3. To make the Italian ketchup, toast the dried chiles in a dry skillet over medium heat until fragrant, 3–4 minutes. Reserve 4 chiles and grind the rest into a powder; set aside the powder for the burgers.

4. Heat a large skillet over high heat, then add the tomatoes, shallot, and garlic. Cook until the tomatoes are blistered and the shallot and garlic are charred. Transfer the tomatoes, shallot, and garlic to a large pot and add the reserved 4 toasted chiles, salt, and sugar. Cover with water and bring to a boil. Cook for 20 minutes, then drain. Put the solids in a blender and blend until smooth, then strain through a fine-mesh strainer.

(recipe continues)

5. Heat the vegetable oil in a large skillet over high heat until smoking. Add the sauce and cook until thick, stirring constantly, about 5 minutes. Set aside.

6. When ready to make the burgers, preheat a grill to high heat.

7. Melt the butter in a small saucepan over low heat. Add 1½ tablespoons of the reserved chile powder and cook for 2 minutes, then remove from the heat.

8. In a large bowl, mix the three meats together, then add the chile butter and mix thoroughly. Form into six equal patties.

9. Heat a 12-inch cast iron skillet on the grill. Add three burgers and cook about 3 minutes until a charred crust develops on the bottom, then flip the burgers over and place a piece of cheese on each. When the cheese starts to melt, add a small amount of water to the skillet and cover with aluminum foil. Cook for 4 more minutes for medium-rare, or to your desired doneness. Transfer the burgers to a plate and repeat with the remaining burgers and cheese.

10. While the burgers are cooking, make the arugula insalata. In a bowl, whisk together the lemon juice, salt, and pepper. Add the arugula and toss to coat. Add 1 tablespoon of the Calabrian chile oil and toss again.

11. Spread 1½ tablespoons of the Italian ketchup on both halves of each roll. Place a burger on the bottom half, along with some of the crispy cheese from the skillet, then spread a little more ketchup on top. Add ¼ cup of the arugula insalata, then 2 pieces of crispy prosciutto. Close with the top roll and serve.

Crowd–Pleaser Tostadas

Silvia

Tostadas are perfect for large gatherings because your guests, from meat eaters to vegetarians to vegans, can customize their own dishes to their personal tastes. Layers of meat (or not!), beans, vegetables, and salsa create a surprisingly complex flavor profile. Take the time to season each layer so your tostadas will taste as spectacular as they look. **Serves 6**

Salsa

4 tomatillos

2 Roma tomatoes

2 serrano peppers

¼ white onion

1 teaspoon salt

1 teaspoon dried Mexican oregano

Tostadas

1 boneless, skinless chicken breast

2 garlic cloves, peeled

½ white onion

6 cilantro sprigs, plus more chopped cilantro for garnish

1 bay leaf

5 whole black peppercorns

1½ teaspoons salt, plus more to taste

1 white potato

1 large carrot

1 tablespoon vegetable oil

1 (16-ounce) can pinto beans

Ground black pepper to taste

2 medium avocados

6 tostada shells

1 head iceberg lettuce, sliced

2 tomatoes, sliced

10 ounces queso fresco, crumbled

Crema Mexicana (Mexican-style sour cream) to taste

1. In a cast iron skillet or comal, roast the tomatillos, tomatoes, peppers, and onion over high heat, turning often, until soft, 10–12 minutes. Remove the serrano stems and put all the vegetables in a blender. Add the salt and oregano and blend until smooth. Add a little bit of water if needed. Set aside.

2. Put the chicken, garlic, onion, cilantro, bay leaf, peppercorns, and salt in a medium pot, cover with water, and bring to a boil over high heat. Lower the heat to medium and cook for 20 minutes, or until the chicken is tender. Transfer the chicken to a cutting board; discard the other ingredients in the pot. When cool enough to handle, shred the chicken.

3. Meanwhile, put the potato and carrot in another pot, cover with water, and bring to a boil over high heat. Lower the heat to medium-high and cook for 20 minutes, or until the potato and carrot are tender but still firm. Transfer the potato and carrot to a cutting board. When cool enough to handle, peel and slice the potato and carrot.

(recipe continues)

4. Heat the oil in a large skillet over high heat. Empty the can of beans into the skillet and mash them with their juices. Lower the heat to medium-high and stir until the beans are completely blended and thickened a bit, about 10 minutes. Season with salt and pepper if needed. Set aside.

5. When ready to serve, peel, pit, and slice the avocados. Spread a layer of beans on a tostada, then add a layer of chopped lettuce, 1–2 slices of tomato, 3–4 slices of carrot, and 1 slice of potato. Add some chicken and avocado and finish with a generous helping of queso fresco, crema, and salsa. Garnish with cilantro and serve.

Tri-Tip Tacos

Silvia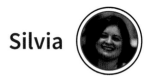

I wanted to create a dish that represents my past and my present, a perfect pairing of the place where I was born, Mexico, and the place where I live now, San Luis Obispo, California. I'm delighted with the result. Tri-tip is a local specialty of California's Central Coast and is the centerpiece of a Santa María–style barbecue, where the triangular cut of beef is seasoned with a dry rub, grilled over oak wood, and served in slices with salsa, green salad, and beans. Here, all the flavors of a Santa María barbecue are wrapped up in a street taco.

Serves 8 (24 tacos total)

Meat

1 tablespoon celery salt

1 tablespoon onion powder

1 tablespoon dried minced garlic

1 tablespoon ground black pepper

1 tablespoon dried oregano

½ teaspoon cayenne pepper

1 (2-pound) tri-tip steak, at room temperature

3 tablespoons olive oil

Pickled onions

1 red onion, thinly sliced

1 cup orange juice

½ cup white vinegar

2 teaspoons salt

1 teaspoon dried Mexican oregano

Avocado salsa

1 pound tomatillos

3 serrano peppers, stemmed

½ white onion

1 large bunch cilantro

1 teaspoon salt

1 medium avocado, peeled and pitted

Tacos

24 (5-inch/taco-size) corn tortillas

1 head iceberg lettuce, thinly sliced

10 ounces queso fresco, crumbled

4 limes, cut into wedges

1. Preheat the oven to 400 degrees F.

2. Mix the celery salt, onion powder, minced garlic, black pepper, oregano, and cayenne. Sprinkle the tri-tip with the rub, massaging the meat all over. Set aside to rest for 10 minutes.

3. Heat the oil in a cast iron skillet over medium-high heat and sear the meat, starting with the fat side down, for 1–2 minutes per side. Transfer the skillet to the oven and roast for 15–20 minutes per pound, or until a thermometer reaches 130 degrees F when inserted in the center (for medium-rare). Cover the meat with aluminum foil and rest for 10–20 minutes. Slice against the grain, then chop into small pieces.

4. Meanwhile, put the red onion in a medium bowl. Cover with warm water and let sit for 10 minutes. In a separate bowl, whisk together the orange juice, vinegar, salt, and oregano. Drain the onion and return it to the bowl. Pour the vinegar mixture over the onion, cover, and set aside for 30 minutes.

5. Combine the tomatillos, serrano peppers, and onion in a small saucepan, cover with water, and bring to a boil over high heat. Turn the heat down and simmer for 5 minutes. Drain the vegetables and let cool for 10–15 minutes. Blend the tomatillos, serrano peppers, onion, cilantro, salt, and avocado until smooth.

6. Warm up the tortillas in a cast iron skillet. To make each taco, place some lettuce on a tortilla, then add the meat, pickled onions, avocado salsa, and queso fresco. Serve with lime wedges for squeezing.

Linguiça Beans (page 31) are also pictured

Beef Parrillada Tacos

Silvia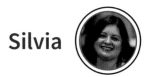

Parrillada means "cookout," and parrillada tacos feature prominently at our family barbecue gatherings. The meat is marinated in Mexican beer, lime juice, and spices, then grilled, chopped, and mixed with tender bell peppers and onions. Serve it with guacamole, chile de árbol salsa, and my Linguiça Beans (page 31) on the side. One bite and you won't be able to stop. **Serves 6 (20 tacos total)**

Salsa

8 ounces tomatillos

8 ounces Roma tomatoes

½ medium white onion

3 jalapeños

6 dried chiles de árbol

1 teaspoon salt

1 teaspoon dried oregano

Tacos

1½ pounds beef skirt steak

2 garlic cloves, finely chopped

1 tablespoon Worcestershire sauce

Juice of 1 lime, plus lime wedges for serving

1 teaspoon salt

1 teaspoon ground black pepper

½ teaspoon cayenne pepper

½ teaspoon paprika

2 (12-ounce) bottles Mexican beer

1 tablespoon olive or vegetable oil

1 medium white onion, chopped

1 red bell pepper, seeded and chopped

1 yellow bell pepper, seeded and chopped

1 green bell pepper, seeded and chopped

20 (5-inch/taco-size) corn tortillas, warmed

Fresh cilantro leaves, for garnish

10 ounces queso fresco, crumbled

Guacamole

3 ripe avocados

¼ white onion, chopped

2 serrano peppers, minced

1 bunch cilantro, chopped, reserve a few leaves for garnish

Juice of 1 lime

Salt to taste

1. In a cast iron skillet or comal, roast the tomatillos, tomatoes, onion, and jalapeños over medium-high heat, turning often, until soft, 10–12 minutes. Remove the seeds from the chiles de árbol and roast for a few seconds just to release the aroma and flavor. Transfer the chiles to a small bowl, cover with boiling water, and let them rehydrate for 20 minutes, then drain. Put the tomatillos, tomatoes, onion, jalapeños, chiles de árbol, salt, and oregano in a blender and blend until smooth. Pour the salsa into a bowl.

2. Meanwhile, put the steak in a large bowl and season with the garlic, Worcestershire sauce, lime juice, salt, black pepper, cayenne pepper, and paprika. Pour in the beer, mix well, and set aside to marinate for 15 minutes.

3. Heat the oil in a Dutch oven over medium heat. Add the onion and cook until soft, about 3 minutes. Add the bell peppers and cook until soft, about 10 minutes. Set aside.

4. Drain the steak and pat it dry. Cook the steak in a cast iron grill pan over medium-high heat until cooked through, about 3 minutes per side. Let it rest for 10 minutes, then add it to the onion-pepper mixture.

5. When ready to serve, peel, pit, and chop the avocados. In a bowl, combine the avocados, onion, serrano peppers, cilantro, lime juice, and salt. Mash all the ingredients together.

6. Serve the parrillada mixture in tortillas with salsa, guacamole, cilantro leaves, and queso fresco. Serve with lime wedges.

Korean Chicken Tacos

Tony

As someone born in Korea and raised in the United States, I did not grow up having a clear connection to Korea. I gravitated toward chefs like Roy Choi because of their fusion cooking and looked up to them because of how they created their own way of expressing their identity through food. This is my version of chicken tacos: spicy, sweet gochujang-marinated chicken topped with fermented kimchi. Blending Korean flavors with Mexican flair, these tacos are for sure a favorite for any gathering. **Serves 6**

½ cup gochujang

⅓ cup plus 2 tablespoons soy sauce, divided

6 tablespoons vegetable oil, divided

5 tablespoons toasted sesame oil, divided

¼ cup maple syrup or honey

3 tablespoons hot chili oil or garlic chili sauce

2 tablespoons rice wine vinegar

1 (2-inch) knob ginger, grated

4 garlic cloves, minced

1 teaspoon salt

1 teaspoon ground black pepper

Gochugaru (Korean red pepper flakes) to taste (optional)

3 pounds boneless, skinless chicken thighs

6 (8-inch) flour tortillas

½ teaspoon sesame seeds

1 (14-ounce) jar kimchi, drained and roughly chopped

3 scallions, thinly sliced on the bias

---

1. In a large bowl, whisk together the gochujang, ⅓ cup of the soy sauce, 2 tablespoons of the vegetable oil, 3 tablespoons of the sesame oil, the maple syrup, chili oil, vinegar, ginger, garlic, salt, pepper, and gochugaru (if using). Taste and adjust the seasoning if needed. Add the chicken thighs to the bowl and toss to coat. Cover and marinate in the refrigerator for 30 minutes or up to 2 hours.

2. Heat 2 tablespoons of the vegetable oil in a large skillet or grill pan over medium-high heat. Working in batches, add the chicken and cook, turning occasionally and brushing with the marinade, until the internal temperature registers 165 degrees F, 7–10 minutes. Transfer the chicken to a plate as it is cooked, and add more oil as needed for the remaining batches. Cut the chicken into bite-size pieces, then transfer to a clean bowl.

3. Place the tortillas on a grill or grill pan and char lightly on both sides, or microwave for 20 seconds to heat through.

4. To make the dipping sauce, in a small bowl, whisk together the remaining 2 tablespoons soy sauce, remaining 2 tablespoons sesame oil, and sesame seeds.

5. To serve, top each tortilla with some of the chicken, add some kimchi, and garnish with scallions. Serve the dipping sauce with the tacos.

Shrimp Tacos

with Chips and Salsa

Nikki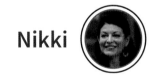

Kids will love these light, fresh, and crisp tacos, perfect for a family dinner. This recipe is special to my family. When I was pregnant with my youngest, he was overdue. Instead of inducing labor, we ate a big Mexican feast (including tacos!) and he was born later that day. It's now a family tradition to eat tacos every year on his birthday, and we love preparing this meal together. **Serves 4**

Pico

1 avocado, peeled, pitted, and diced

2 Roma tomatoes, diced

1 bunch cilantro, chopped

1 red onion, diced

Juice of 2 limes

Pinch sea salt

Crema

¼ cup chopped scallions

¼ cup chopped fresh cilantro

2 garlic cloves, minced

1 large jalapeño, minced

¼ cup plain Greek yogurt

1½ teaspoons grated lime zest

1½ teaspoons fresh lime juice

¼ teaspoon sea salt

Salsa

1 (28-ounce) can whole tomatoes

½ cup chopped yellow onion

1 bunch cilantro

1 jalapeño

1–2 tablespoons fresh lime juice

2 teaspoons ground cumin

1 teaspoon sea salt

Shrimp

Juice of 1 lemon

1 tablespoon chili powder

1 tablespoon ground cumin

1 teaspoon ground coriander

Pinch salt

2 garlic cloves, minced

½ cup plus 2 tablespoons olive oil

1 pound large shrimp, peeled and deveined

Chips

½ cup vegetable oil

6 large flour tortillas, cut into triangles

Tacos

8 corn tortillas

2 cups shredded red and green cabbage

¼ cup chopped fresh cilantro

2 avocados, sliced

2 limes, cut into wedges

1. In a small bowl, combine all the pico ingredients and mix well. Set aside.

2. In another small bowl, combine all the crema ingredients and mix well. Set aside.

3. In a blender, combine all the salsa ingredients and blend until not completely smooth, with a little chunkiness remaining. Transfer to a medium bowl and set aside.

4. To make the shrimp marinade, in a large bowl, whisk together the lemon juice, chili powder, cumin, coriander, salt, garlic, and ½ cup of the olive oil. Add the shrimp and toss to coat. Set aside to marinate while you make the chips.

5. Heat the vegetable oil in a large skillet over medium-high heat. Add the flour tortilla triangles and fry until browned and crispy. Using tongs, transfer the chips to paper towels and set aside.

6. In the same skillet, heat the remaining 2 tablespoons olive oil over medium-high heat. Add the shrimp and cook until opaque, 4–6 minutes. Cut the shrimp in half lengthwise.

7. Warm the corn tortillas in a skillet or over the stovetop flame. Layer each tortilla with shrimp, shredded cabbage, avocado, pico, and crema. Garnish with cilantro and lime wedges for squeezing.

8. Serve with chips, salsa, and additional pico.

Pizza Calabrese

Dan

The world loves pizza (or "pizz-er" as we say in Rhode Island)! I say it doesn't matter who you are, there is nothing more comforting and satisfying than a slice of pizza, and this recipe is for one of my favorites. It's easy, it's hot, and it's satisfying on a fundamental level, especially after working long hours. Pretty much everything I cook has a lineage in my family—even the pizz-er. My uncle David gave me his pizza sheet tray to use on *The Great American Recipe* to ensure the family spirit came through in this challenge. This recipe is for one of my favorites—pizza with spicy Italian deli salami. **Serves 8**

---

2 pounds pizza dough

1 (28-ounce) can whole San Marzano tomatoes

2 tablespoons olive oil, divided

1 garlic clove, crushed

1 teaspoon dried oregano

½ teaspoon kosher salt, plus more for seasoning

¼ teaspoon ground black pepper, plus more for seasoning

⅛ teaspoon red pepper flakes

All-purpose flour, for dusting

20 thin slices Calabrese hot salami

2 (25-ounce) balls buffalo mozzarella, sliced and patted dry

2 cups arugula, for garnish

2 tablespoons Calabrian chile oil

2 teaspoons grated Pecorino Romano cheese

---

1. Preheat the oven to 450 degrees F.

2. Take the dough out of the refrigerator and let it rest while you make the sauce.

3. Blend the tomatoes with their juices in a blender until smooth.

4. Heat 1 tablespoon of the olive oil in a saucepan over medium heat. Add the garlic and cook until just browned. Add the tomato puree, oregano, salt, black pepper, and red pepper flakes. Bring the sauce to a simmer, then turn off the heat.

5. Brush a rimmed baking sheet with the remaining 1 tablespoon olive oil. Dust your fingers with flour to prevent sticking, then spread out the dough on the baking sheet. Top the dough with the sauce, sliced salami, and sliced mozzarella.

6. Bake for 10 minutes, then rotate the baking sheet and bake for an another 10 minutes.

7. While the pizza is in the oven, put the arugula in a bowl, season with salt and pepper, drizzle with the chile oil, and toss to mix.

8. Take the pizza out of the oven. Add the arugula salad on top of the pizza, then top with the Pecorino Romano. Cut into 8 slices and serve.

Pesto Pizza

Silvia

I love making pizza with my husband. In our home, we trade responsibilities—he cooks one week and I cook the next—but every Friday we make pizza together. He introduced me to pesto the first time I visited California and since then we've made it often at home. Keep the color and freshness of the pesto by adding it right before serving the pizza. This recipe is perfect for those days when you don't have a lot of time. Thanks to the use of fast-acting yeast, the dough needs just 10 minutes of resting time. **Serves 4**

Roasted tomatoes

1 pint mixed cherry tomatoes, halved

1 tablespoon extra-virgin olive oil

¼ teaspoon kosher salt

Ground black pepper to taste

Pizza

2¼ cups bread flour, plus more
for dusting

1 teaspoon kosher salt

1 teaspoon dried basil

1 teaspoon dried Mexican oregano

1 garlic clove, minced

2¼ teaspoons fast-acting instant yeast

1½ teaspoons sugar

⅔ cup warm water (120–130°F)

3 tablespoons olive oil

Fine cornmeal, for dusting

1 cup mozzarella cheese, shredded

1 cup Oaxaca cheese, shredded

½ teaspoon garlic salt

Pesto

3 cups packed fresh basil leaves, plus
more for garnish

1 garlic clove, peeled

½ cup pine nuts, plus more for garnish

¾ cup grated Pecorino Romano cheese

½ cup extra virgin olive oil

½ teaspoon kosher salt

Ground black pepper to taste

1. Preheat the oven to 400 degrees F.

2. On a rimmed baking sheet, toss the cherry tomatoes with the olive oil, salt, and pepper. Spread them out and roast for 25 minutes. Remove the sheet from the oven and set aside. Increase the temperature to 500 degrees F.

3. In the bowl of a mixer with the bread hook attachment, combine the flour, salt, basil, oregano, and garlic. Using your hands or a fork, give it a quick mix. Add the yeast and sugar and mix again. Add the water and oil and mix at medium speed until the dough is smooth and elastic, about 4 minutes. Cover and let the dough rest for 10 minutes.

4. Spread a thin layer of cornmeal on a pizza peel and place the pizza dough on top. Using your hands, form the dough into a round.

5. Scatter the mozzarella and Oaxaca cheeses on top, leaving a rim around the edge, then sprinkle the garlic salt on the rim. Transfer to a pizza stone in the oven and bake for 15 minutes, or until the crust is golden brown and the cheese is melted.

6. Meanwhile, in a food processor, combine the basil, garlic, pine nuts, Pecorino Romano cheese, olive oil, salt, and pepper. Mix until well blended. Scrape down the mixture from the sides. Taste and add more salt and pepper if needed.

7. Just before serving, spread the pesto on top of the cheese pizza, add the roasted tomatoes, and garnish with fresh basil leaves.

Family Dinners

Leah's Crowd–Pleasing Thai Grilled Chicken with Corn Salad

Leah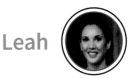

If I were to pick one city in the world to live in (aside from NYC), it would have to be Bangkok. I love the city's street food scene—some of the best meals I have eaten came from a street food vendor who specialized in three or four dishes. Traditionally, this dish (gai yang) would be prepared with the chicken spatchcocked and grilled over charcoal. A classic pairing is som tum (papaya salad), but the salad can be made with many other ingredients, like corn, which is what I've used here. If the street vendor preparing the grilled chicken isn't also serving the salad, look to the vendor next door because they will most likely be making it. I highly suggest serving this with sticky rice. **Serves 4**

Chicken

¼ cup cilantro stems

8 garlic cloves, peeled

½ cup palm sugar

2 tablespoons fish sauce

2 tablespoons oyster sauce

½ teaspoon ground turmeric

1½ tablespoons whole white peppercorns

4 bone-in, skin-on chicken legs (thigh and drumstick attached)

Garlic oil and crispy garlic

¼ cup vegetable oil

8–10 garlic cloves, minced

Corn salad

6 fresh red Thai chiles

3 garlic cloves, minced

⅓ cup palm sugar

1 cup plus 2 tablespoons fresh lime juice

2 tablespoons fish sauce

1¼ cup corn kernels

½ pound long beans, cut into 1-inch pieces

12 cherry tomatoes, quartered

¼ cup whole peanuts

½ teaspoon salt, plus more to taste

1. Combine the cilantro, garlic, palm sugar, fish sauce, oyster sauce, turmeric, and white peppercorns in a food processor and blend until smooth. Transfer to a large bowl, add the chicken, and turn to coat. Cover and refrigerate for 12 hours.

2. Meanwhile, to make the salad dressing, combine the chiles, garlic, palm sugar, lime juice, and fish sauce in a blender and blend until well mixed but not completely smooth.

3. Bring a large pot of water to a boil. Fill a large bowl with cold water and ice cubes. Add the corn kernels to the boiling water and cook for 5 minutes. Using a slotted spoon or spider, transfer the

(recipe continues)

corn to the ice bath to cool. Add the long beans to the boiling water and blanch for 20 seconds. Using a slotted spoon or spider, transfer the long beans to the ice bath to cool. Drain the corn and long beans.

4. In a large bowl, combine the tomatoes, corn, long beans, peanuts, and salt and gently toss to combine. Add the dressing and toss again. Cover and refrigerate the salad until ready to serve.

5. Preheat a grill to medium-low heat.

6. In a small saucepan, heat the oil over medium heat to 300 degrees F. Add the garlic and cook, stirring constantly, until light golden. Strain, reserving the garlic oil. Save the crispy garlic in an airtight container for another use (see note).

7. Grill the chicken, turning occasionally and brushing with the garlic oil, until cooked through, 25–30 minutes.

8. Serve the chicken with the corn salad.

Note: Looking for a way to use that crispy garlic? Use it as a topping for Carter G's Favorite Chicken Adobo (page 105).

Crispy Chicken Thighs with Herbed Potatoes and Mustard Greens

Tiffany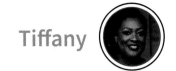

Chicken thighs are budget-friendly and deliver big flavor. Here, you'll baste them with garlic and thyme as they cook, and then use the juices to make an amazing lemony pan sauce. If the chicken is spattering as it cooks, use a lid to partially cover the pan to stop any oil from popping you. Just be sure not to cover the pan completely so the chicken skin stays crispy. **Serves 2**

---

2 boneless, skin-on chicken thighs

1 teaspoon kosher salt, plus more to taste

1 teaspoon ground white pepper, plus more to taste

4 garlic cloves, peeled

2 thyme sprigs

3 tablespoons olive oil

1 tablespoon fish sauce

1 tablespoon grated lemon zest

2 tablespoons fresh lemon juice

Pinch red pepper flakes or 1 Thai chile, thinly sliced

¼ cup chopped fresh cilantro

8 ounces mustard greens, thinly sliced

1 lemon wedge

---

1. Season the chicken thigh skin with ¾ teaspoon salt and sprinkle the remainder on the other side. Sprinkle white pepper on both sides and allow the chicken to sit for 30 minutes. Pat with paper towels to remove excess seasoning and moisture.

2. Place the chicken thighs skin-side down in a cold sauté pan. Turn the heat to medium and allow the chicken skin to get crispy, 10–12 minutes. (Partially cover the pan if the fat is spattering.)

3. Once the skin is crispy and deep golden brown, turn the thighs over. Add the garlic and thyme (be careful, as the thyme will pop slightly when it hits the pan). Baste the chicken with the seasoned oil and cook until an instant-read thermometer inserted into the thickest portion reaches 160 degrees F, about 5 minutes more. Transfer the chicken to a plate, skin-side up.

4. Add the olive oil, fish sauce, lemon zest, lemon juice, and red pepper flakes to the pan drippings and cook for about 30 seconds, stirring well to release any brown bits stuck to the bottom of the pan (the fond). Add the cilantro. Taste and add more salt and pepper as needed.

5. Put the mustard greens in a bowl. Squeeze the lemon wedge over the greens, season with salt and pepper, and toss.

6. Place a crispy chicken thigh and half the mustard greens on each plate. Spoon the sauce over the chicken and greens and serve with the herbed potatoes (recipe follows).

Herbed Potatoes

1 pound small red potatoes, cut in half

1 tablespoon kosher salt, plus more to taste

2 teaspoons unsalted butter

1 teaspoon garlic powder

¼ cup chopped fresh flat-leaf parsley

Ground black pepper to taste

1 lemon wedge

1. Put the potatoes and salt in a medium saucepan and cover with cold water. Bring to a boil and cook until the potatoes are fork-tender, about 20 minutes. Drain the potatoes, then return them to the pan. Add the butter and garlic powder and stir. Add the parsley and a few grindings of black pepper. Taste and adjust the seasoning if needed. Squeeze the lemon wedge over the potatoes just before serving.

Chicken Adobo Bowls

Christina

A traditional Filipino dish, adobo is typically made with a whole chicken, skin-on, or with pork belly. I adapted the recipe to be lower in sodium and fat, used a pressure cooker for the chicken to save time, and added whole grains and vegetables for a well-rounded and nutritious meal. The sweet and tangy sauce gives the bowls that distinctive adobo flavor. You can replace or add to the kale and carrot slaw with other vegetables, such as blanched broccoli, but don't skip the rice—it helps absorb the sauce to keep your bowl from becoming soupy. (Leftover cooked rice is best and makes prep even simpler.) **Serves 4**

Adobo

1 cup apple cider vinegar

1 cup low-sodium soy sauce

½ cup honey or maple syrup

6 garlic cloves, minced

½ teaspoon whole black peppercorns

½ teaspoon coriander seeds

¼ teaspoon red pepper flakes

1–2 tablespoons olive oil

2–3 pounds chicken breasts (can be boneless and skinless, or with bone and skin)

3 bay leaves

Rice

3 tablespoons unsalted butter

2 garlic cloves, minced

2 cups cooked brown rice

2 large eggs, beaten

½ teaspoon lemon pepper seasoning

Slaw

1 tablespoon low-sodium soy sauce

1 tablespoon toasted sesame oil

1 tablespoon rice vinegar

1½ teaspoons honey or maple syrup

1½ cups shredded kale

1½ cups shredded carrot

1. In a small bowl, whisk together the apple cider vinegar, soy sauce, honey, garlic, black peppercorns, coriander, and red pepper flakes.

2. Set a pressure cooker to the sauté function and add the oil. When the oil shimmers, add the chicken and lightly brown on all sides, 5–7 minutes. (Work in batches if necessary.) Transfer the chicken to a plate.

3. Add the vinegar mixture and bay leaves to the pot and deglaze by gently stirring and scraping to loosen any bits stuck to the bottom (this will help avoid the "Burn" notice).

4. Place the lid on the pot, turn to high pressure, and set to 15 minutes.

5. Meanwhile, make the rice. Melt the butter in a large nonstick skillet over medium-low heat. Add the garlic and sauté until fragrant, but don't allow the garlic to brown. Add the rice and stir

(recipe continues)

to incorporate. Add the eggs and lemon pepper seasoning and mix thoroughly. Continue mixing and stirring until the rice is slightly crisped and the eggs are thoroughly cooked.

6. When the rice is finished, make the slaw. In a small bowl, whisk together the soy sauce, sesame oil, rice vinegar, and honey. In a large bowl, mix the kale and carrot until evenly mixed. Pour the dressing onto the kale and carrot mixture and mix by massaging with your hands.

7. When the adobo is done, remove the chicken and place on a plate. While the chicken is cooling, turn the pot to the sauté function and allow the sauce to reduce and thicken. It should be a little more viscous and not as runny. Shred the chicken or cut it into bite-size pieces.

8. To serve, spoon some rice into wide, shallow bowls, layer with the kale-carrot slaw, then top with the chicken. Liberally spoon the sauce over everything.

Carter G's Favorite Chicken Adobo

Leah

Adobo is the most popular Filipino dish out there. Every household debates who makes the best version among their family members, and there's usually one clear winner. In my household, my son Carter named me the winner. He requests that I make this for him once a week, and since it is a simple one-pot dish, I happily agree. Every adobo has to include these five ingredients: soy sauce, garlic, bay leaves, black pepper, and vinegar. The remaining ingredients are up to the cook; the protein is usually chicken or pork. My secret ingredient is coconut milk, which gives the adobo some richness and a hint of sweetness. I think this is what makes my adobo the best in my family. **Serves 6**

4 tablespoons vegetable oil, divided

6 bone-in, skin-on chicken thighs

6 bone-in, skin-on chicken drumsticks

1 large Spanish onion, halved and thinly sliced

6 garlic cloves, minced

1 cup low-sodium soy sauce

1 cup water

½ cup canned coconut milk

½ cup coconut vinegar or apple cider vinegar

3 tablespoons sugar

1 tablespoon ground black pepper

8 bay leaves

Steamed jasmine rice, for serving

2 tablespoons crispy garlic (see note)

2 scallions, thinly sliced

1. Heat 2 tablespoons of the oil in a large Dutch oven over high heat until the oil begins to shimmer. Add the chicken thighs and cook until golden brown on both sides, about 3 minutes per side. Transfer to a large plate.

2. Add the remaining 2 tablespoons oil to the pan and heat until the oil shimmers. Add the chicken drumsticks and cook until golden brown on both sides, about 3 minutes per side. Transfer to the plate with the thighs.

3. Pour off all but 2 tablespoons of the fat from the pan; add the onion and cook, stirring occasionally, until soft, about 5 minutes.

4. Add the garlic, soy sauce, water, coconut milk, vinegar, sugar, pepper, and bay leaves and stir until combined. Return the chicken to the pot and bring to a boil. Reduce the heat to low, cover, and cook until the chicken is tender, about 1 hour. If the liquid reduces too quickly or becomes too salty, add a bit more water.

5. Remove the bay leaves. Serve with steamed jasmine rice, garnished with the crispy garlic and scallions.

Note: To make your own crispy garlic, refer to the recipe in Leah's Crowd-Pleasing Thai Grilled Chicken with Corn Salad (page 97). You can use store-bought crispy garlic but it doesn't taste nearly as good.

Hungarian Chicken Paprikash with Nokedli (Dumplings)

Brian

Making chicken paprikash was a ritual in my family: my great-grandfather learned how to make this dish from his great-grandfather, and I learned it from my grandmother. The creamy and peppery sauce creates a perfect bite with the tender chicken and fluffy Hungarian dumplings, called nokedli. This is the perfect hearty meal to feed your family and warm your bones on a cold winter day. This dish is made with a lot of care and love, which you will taste in every bite. **Serves 4**

Paprikash

2 tablespoons vegetable oil

3 pounds bone-in, skin-on chicken thighs

1 medium yellow onion, diced

1 (4-ounce) jar roasted red bell peppers, drained and diced

2 garlic cloves, minced

2 tablespoons all-purpose flour

¼ cup Hungarian paprika

2 teaspoons salt

2 cups chicken broth

½ cup sour cream

Chopped fresh flat-leaf parsley, for garnish

Nokedli

4 tablespoons salt, divided

1 tablespoon white vinegar

2 cups all-purpose flour

4 large eggs, beaten

¼ cup milk

2 teaspoons ground white pepper

1. Heat the oil in a Dutch oven over medium heat until shimmering. Working in batches if necessary, place the chicken into the pot skin-side down. Sear for 5–7 minutes, then flip them over and brown the other side, 5–7 minutes more. Transfer the chicken thighs to a plate.

2. Add the onion, roasted red peppers, and garlic to the pot and sauté for 5 minutes. Add the flour and whisk to create a roux, cooking it to a dirty-blond color. Remove the pot from the heat to prevent scorching of the spices. Stir in the paprika and salt, letting the paprika bloom in the oil.

3. Return the chicken to the pot and cover with the chicken broth. Simmer over medium-low heat for 40 minutes.

4. Transfer the chicken to a clean plate. Once the chicken is cool enough to handle, remove the skin and bones and cut the meat into bite-size pieces. Return the meat to the pot and stir it in.

5. When the paprikash is almost done, make the nokedli. Fill a large pot with water and add 3 tablespoons of the salt and the vinegar. Bring the water to a boil.

6. In a large bowl, mix the flour, eggs, milk, white pepper, and remaining 1 tablespoon salt together until combined.

7. Spray a colander with nonstick cooking spray. Put the dough in the colander and, using a spoon, push the dough through the colander into the boiling water. Cook the dumplings until they float to the surface, indicating that they are done, about 2–3 minutes. Remove with a slotted spoon and transfer to a bowl.

8. Pile the nokedli on each serving plate, add a ladleful of chicken paprikash, and garnish with a dollop of sour cream and some parsley.

Chicken Congee

Foo

This light and simple rice porridge is soulful and comforting. The deep chicken broth, with subtle hints of grilled ginger and onion, is cooked with toasted jasmine rice and topped with kimchi to give the congee some salt and acid. Serve it alongside a crispy Chinese long doughnut, which you can find frozen in specialty stores or online, to be used as a dipping vehicle for the scrumptious congee. **Serves 4**

Congee

1 cup jasmine rice

1 Vidalia onion

1 knob ginger

2 pounds chicken necks

1 pound chicken wings

1 tablespoon fish sauce

4 cups chicken broth

4 cups water

1 tablespoon Chinese rock sugar (see note on page 54)

2 teaspoons salt

1 tablespoon whole black peppercorns

4 Chinese long doughnuts

1 bunch scallions, sliced

3 tablespoons minced kimchi

Broth

4 cups chicken broth

8 cups water

1 tablespoon fish sauce

1 tablespoon Chinese rock sugar (see note on page 54)

1 pound chicken necks

1 pound chicken wings

1 pound bone-in, skin-on chicken breasts

1. Preheat the oven to 250 degrees F.

2. Spread out the rice on a rimmed baking sheet and bake for 10 minutes. Set aside. Raise the oven temperature to 300 degrees F.

3. Char the onion and ginger over the stovetop flame (or on a grill) until blackened and aromatic. Put the onion and ginger in a pressure cooker, then add the chicken necks, chicken wings, fish sauce, chicken broth, water, rock sugar, salt, and peppercorns. Set the pressure cooker on high for 30 minutes.

4. Meanwhile, make the broth. In a large pot, combine the chicken broth, water, fish sauce, rock sugar, chicken necks, chicken wings, and chicken breasts and bring to a boil. Boil for 20 minutes. Transfer the chicken breasts to a plate. Discard the chicken wings and necks.

5. When the pressure cooker is finished, strain the contents and add the strained broth to the pot on the stove. (Discard the solids.) Add the toasted rice and gently stir the congee. Cook over medium heat for 10 minutes.

6. When the chicken breasts are cool enough to handle, discard the skin and bones and slice the meat; set aside.

7. Place the Chinese long doughnuts on a rimmed baking sheet and bake for 15 minutes.

8. Ladle the congee into soup bowls and fan out 4 slices of chicken breast on top of each serving. Garnish with the scallions and about 2 teaspoons of kimchi per bowl. Serve with a crunchy long doughnut alongside.

Cacio e Pepe con Pollo

Dan

Cheese and Pepper Pasta with Chicken

My cacio e pepe (the name means "cheese and pepper") is a homegrown pasta dish that anyone can make. Cacio e pepe is often a very straightforward dish—pasta, cheese, seasonings—but I like to toss mine with cubed chicken and top it with crispy guanciale to make it even more satisfying. People love the simplicity and flavor of this dish, and I'm often asked to share the recipe. I always say, "If you can boil water and you can cook chicken, you can make this at home." This uncomplicated recipe has just a handful of ingredients and can be made quickly; it's best enjoyed immediately. **Serves 4**

---

1 tablespoon vegetable oil

12 ounces guanciale (pork cheek), diced small

4 boneless, skinless chicken breasts, cut into bite-size pieces

¼ teaspoon kosher salt, plus more for cooking the pasta

1 pound linguine fini pasta

2 teaspoons ground black pepper

3 tablespoons Pecorino Romano cheese, plus more for serving

3 tablespoons Parmigiano-Reggiano cheese

---

1. Heat the oil in a large skillet over medium heat. Add the guanciale and cook until slightly crispy but still soft in the center, 8–10 minutes. Transfer to paper towels.

2. Season the chicken with the salt, add it to the skillet, and cook until cooked through, 5–7 minutes. Transfer the chicken to a plate. Reserve the skillet.

3. Bring a large pot of salted water to a boil. Add the pasta and cook for 2 minutes less than the package instructions. When there are 5 minutes left for the pasta to cook, turn the heat under the skillet to low and add the pepper just to toast.

4. Using a glass measuring cup, scoop out 1½ cups of the pasta cooking water and add it to the skillet to deglaze. Remove the pasta with tongs and add it to the skillet, then add both cheeses and the chicken and toss to coat everything and finish cooking.

5. Serve some of the linguine and chicken on each plate, add several pieces of guanciale, and sprinkle another pinch of Pecorino Romano on top.

Mae Emma's Honey Turkey Wings

and Smoked Turkey Cabbage

 Bambi

My mother, Mae Emma, always had her freezer full of turkey wings! They were her favorite food. And no other food connects me more to my Mae Emma—I grew up on these honey turkey wings, so this recipe is like the origin story of my cooking. The aroma of turkey, cabbage, and corn bread will evoke strong memories of just about any Southern home, and this hearty dish will pack your plate with "go big or go home" flavor. **Serves 6**

Turkey wings

½ cup fresh lemon juice

6 turkey wings

¼ cup brown sugar

2 tablespoons salt-free seasoning blend, such as Dash

2 tablespoons garlic powder

2 tablespoons dried minced onion

1 tablespoon onion powder

1 tablespoon smoked paprika

1 tablespoon lemon pepper seasoning

2 teaspoons dried minced garlic

1 teaspoon ground mustard

1 teaspoon red pepper flakes

½ teaspoon poultry seasoning

8 tablespoons (1 stick) salted butter, at room temperature

½ teaspoon chicken bouillon powder

1 cup water

1 large onion, sliced

½ cup honey, divided

Smoked turkey cabbage

¼ cup olive oil

1 cup chopped red bell pepper

1 smoked turkey wing

2 tablespoons salt-free seasoning blend, such as Dash

2 teaspoons chicken bouillon powder

Seasoning salt, such as Lawry's, to taste

1 medium head cabbage, cored and chopped

½ cup sugar

4 thick slices bacon, cooked and crumbled

---

1. Preheat the oven to 400 degrees F.

2. Fill a large bowl with cold water and add the lemon juice. Rinse the turkey wings in the lemon water and drip dry. Empty the bowl and put the wings back in.

3. In a small bowl, mix the brown sugar, salt-free seasoning, garlic powder, minced onion, onion powder, smoked paprika, lemon pepper seasoning, minced garlic, mustard, red pepper flakes, and poultry seasoning. Set aside half of the seasoning mixture and rub the remaining half into the wings.

4. Rub the butter all over the wings, even going under the skin, making sure the seasoning stays on the wings while rubbing. Add the remainder of the seasoning to the wings and toss well.

5. In a medium bowl, whisk the chicken bouillon into the water.

(recipe continues)

6. Spread out the sliced onion in a deep roasting pan. Add the wings on top of the onion, then drizzle half of the honey over the wings. Pour the broth mixture along the sides of the pan, making sure not to pour any on top of the wings.

7. Cover the pan with aluminum foil. Cut two small holes through the foil. Bake for 30 minutes, then carefully uncover the pan, baste the wings with the pan juices, cover again, and bake for another 30 minutes. Remove the foil and carefully pour off any pan juices (you can also use a turkey baster to remove them). Glaze the wings with the remaining honey on both sides. Return them to the oven and bake, uncovered, for 20–25 minutes, until the meat is cooked through and falls off the bone.

8. Heat the olive oil in a large skillet over medium heat. Add bell pepper and saute until tender, about 10 minutes.

9. While the turkey wings are baking, fill a large pot halfway filled with water. Add the smoked turkey wing, seasoning blend, chicken bouillon, and seasoning salt. Cover and bring to a rolling bowl, then turn down the heat and simmer for 1 hour. Remove the smoked turkey wing and set aside.

10. Add the cabbage and sugar to the pot and cook over low heat, stirring occasionally, until the cabbage begins to shrink, about 10 minutes. Return the smoked turkey wing to the pot. Add the sautéed bell pepper and bacon. Cover and cook until the cabbage is tender, 10–15 more minutes.

11. To serve, spoon some of the cabbage onto each plate and top with a turkey wing.

Ginger–Soy Glazed Chicken with Mango Salsa

Graham

This is a light, simple dish that packs a big punch when it comes to flavor. Spending my formative years in Hawaii and the Philippines inspired this dish with its use of ginger, soy, and mango. When it comes to tropical fruits, feel free to substitute papaya, guava, or any other flavor that is in season. **Serves 4**

1⅓ pounds boneless skinless chicken breasts

¼ cup low-sodium soy sauce (or coconut aminos)

2 tablespoons orange juice

1 tablespoon sesame oil

1 tablespoon minced fresh ginger

2 garlic cloves, minced

½ teaspoon black pepper, plus more to taste

1 ripe mango, chopped

¼ cup chopped red onion

¼ cup chopped cilantro

Juice of 1 lime

Salt to taste

1. Cut the chicken breasts into thinner cutlets by slicing the breasts in half horizontally. Combine the chicken, soy sauce, orange juice, sesame oil, ginger, garlic, and pepper in an airtight resealable plastic bag. Marinate for 4 hours or more in the fridge.

2. In a medium bowl, toss together the mango, red onion, cilantro, and lime juice. Season with salt and pepper. Allow the flavors to meld while you cook the chicken.

3. When ready to grill, remove the chicken from the marinade, letting excess marinade drip off. Heat a grill to medium-high. Grill for 3–5 minutes per side, or until cooked through.

4. Serve the salsa over the grilled chicken.

Braised Beef Short Ribs with Fingerling Potatoes, Asparagus, and Mushroom Puree

Graham

An all-American classic, updated and elevated. My mom was, how do you say, "limited" in her culinary skills; however, she knew how to throw down when it came to meat and potatoes. Thus, the inspiration for this dish is childhood. This recipe can also be switched up to a grilled steak (ribeye, filet, strip) if you so desire, and the potatoes can be fried, mashed, or any number of other ways. **Serves 4**

Short ribs

2 pounds boneless beef short ribs

Salt and pepper

2 tablespoons vegetable oil

1 large onion, chopped

1 medium carrot, peeled and chopped

1 celery stalk, chopped

4 garlic cloves, minced

5 sprigs thyme

1 tablespoon all-purpose flour

2 (12-ounce) bottles beer
  (I like Guiness here)

3 cups beef broth

Potatoes

8 ounces fingerling potatoes, halved

2 tablespoons olive oil

Salt and pepper

1 sprig fresh rosemary, stemmed and
  chopped

Mushroom puree

1 tablespoon olive oil

½ large onion, diced

2 garlic cloves, minced

8 ounces oyster mushrooms

2 cups mushroom stock

Asparagus

1 tablespoon olive oil

8 ounces asparagus

Salt and pepper

1. Preheat the oven to 300°F.

2. Season the short ribs on both sides with salt and pepper. Heat the oil in a large oven-safe pot or Dutch oven over medium-high heat. Sear the short ribs on all sides, about 2 minutes per side, working in batches if needed to avoid crowding the pot. Remove the short ribs and set aside. Add the onion, carrot, celery garlic, and thyme and sauté for 2 minutes until slightly softened. Add the flour and stir until it evenly coats the vegetables and thickens. Return the short ribs to the pot, cover with the beer and broth, and bring to a boil. Remove from heat, cover with a lid, and transfer to the oven. Cook till tender, 3 hours or so.

3. In the last half hour of cooking, increase the oven temperature to 350°F. Toss the potatoes in 2 tablespoons olive oil, salt, and pepper and arrange on a rimmed baking sheet. Sprinkle the potatoes with rosemary. Roast for 20 minutes until tender. Turn off the oven and keep the potatoes warm inside until you're ready to plate.

4. Meanwhile, make the mushroom puree. Heat 1 tablespoon olive oil in a large sauté pan over medium heat. Sauté the onion and garlic for 2 to 3 minutes until translucent. Add the mushrooms and sauté for 5 minutes until soft. Add the mushroom stock and simmer for 10 minutes. Turn off the heat and allow to cool for 10 minutes, then pour the contents into a blender and puree until smooth. Set aside.

5. Season the sparagus with salt and pepper. Toss in olive oil and place on a grill or grill pan over medium-high heat. Cook for 2–3 minutes, turn, and cook for 2–3 minutes more until crisp-tender. Remove from heat.

6. To assemble, place some mushroom puree in the center of each plate, then top with potatoes. Gently top with braised short ribs, then lean a few asparagus spears on the short rib–potato mix. Feel free to reduce some of the short rib cooking liquid on the stove until it reduces to a sauce-like consistency, then drizzle on and around the short ribs.

Pork Ragù with Polenta

Nikki

Nothing says comfort like rich, creamy ragù and polenta, and this version gets you all that goodness in much less time. Like any true Italian, I can pull together a tomato sauce in a jiffy. As a mom and an entrepreneur, I have learned that I can save time by making dinners using a pressure cooker, so I use one for this recipe. This is a great dish for anyone who is busy and needs to feed a family! **Serves 6**

Pork ragù

1 (2-pound) pork roast

1 teaspoon coarse sea salt

1 teaspoon ground black pepper

1 small yellow onion, sliced

1 fennel bulb, sliced

2 carrots, sliced

2 celery stalks, sliced

6 garlic cloves, sliced

1 (28-ounce) can diced San Marzano tomatoes

1 bay leaf

1 tablespoon dried oregano

1 tablespoon dried Italian seasoning

1 tablespoon dried basil

½ teaspoon red pepper flakes

1 cup dry red wine

Chopped fresh parsley, for garnish

Polenta

4 cups water

1 cup polenta

Pinch sea salt

½ cup grated Parmesan cheese, divided

1. Sprinkle the pork roast with the salt and pepper.

2. Set the pressure cooker to the sauté function. Add the onion, fennel, carrots, celery, and garlic and sauté for 2–3 minutes. Add the pork roast and sear on all sides until browned. Add the tomatoes with their juices, bay leaf, oregano, Italian seasoning, basil, red pepper flakes, and red wine. Stir to combine all the ingredients well around the roast. Secure the lid, select "Manual," and set the time for 25 minutes.

3. When the pressure cooker is done, carefully release the pressure and remove the lid. Remove and discard the bay leaf. Using tongs and a carving fork, break up the pork and stir all the ingredients together.

4. While the ragù is cooking, make the polenta. In a medium saucepan, bring the water to a boil. Add the polenta, lower the heat to medium-low, and cook according to package directions, stirring often with a whisk or wooden spoon, until creamy and thickened. Add a pinch of salt and ¼ cup of the Parmesan cheese. If it is too thick, add more water. Turn the heat to low until ready to serve.

5. Ladle 1 cup polenta into each shallow pasta dish and make a crater in the center. Ladle the ragù into the crater. Garnish with the remaining ¼ cup Parmesan cheese and fresh parsley.

Southwestern Char Siu BBQ Ribs

with Mexican Elote Corn and Pickled Cucumbers

BBQ ribs are one of my favorite foods, and this dish is always on the menu when I host a summer cookout back home—but here, the ribs are cooked in a pressure cooker and broiled to get that slow-cooked fall-off-the-bone tenderness in less time. Inspired by Chinese roast duck and char siu (the red rub that goes on Chinese BBQ), this recipe is a delicious fusion of East and West. To make the ribs, I cover them in char siu, cook them, and then coat them with BBQ sauce. To round it out, I serve the ribs alongside elote corn, a side dish made to mimic the flavors of grilled Mexican street corn, and quick pickled cucumbers. This dish highlights three different cuisines and creates a true melting pot of flavor. **Serves 4**

Pickled cucumbers

¼ cup white vinegar

¼ cup rice vinegar

½ cup water

¼ cup sugar

½ teaspoon kosher salt

2 English cucumbers, thinly sliced

Ribs

1 rack St. Louis–style pork ribs

6 tablespoons garlic salt

Salt and ground black pepper

¼ cup char siu sauce

1 cup water

½ cup apple cider vinegar

½ cup orange juice

1 (19.5-ounce) bottle barbecue sauce, such as Jack Daniel's

5 tablespoons sriracha

3 tablespoons hot sauce, such as Frank's RedHot

Elote corn

5 ears white corn, husks and silk removed

1 (12-ounce) jar mayonnaise or Miracle Whip

Juice of 2 limes

2 tablespoons sriracha

1 teaspoon cayenne pepper

1 teaspoon vegetable oil

---

1. To make the pickled cucumbers, combine the white vinegar, rice vinegar, water, sugar, and salt in a bowl and stir until the sugar and salt dissolve. Add the cucumbers and stir. Cover and refrigerate for 30 minutes.

2. Rub the rack of ribs all over with the garlic salt, salt, pepper, and char siu sauce. Place the ribs in a pressure cooker, add the water, apple cider vinegar, and orange juice, and cook on high pressure for 30 minutes.

3. Combine the barbecue sauce, sriracha, and hot sauce in a bowl and mix well. Preheat the oven broiler on high.

(recipe continues)

4. When the pressure cooker is finished, remove the ribs and slather them with the barbecue sauce mixture. Place the ribs on a rimmed baking sheet and broil for 15 minutes, turning them a few times to char evenly. Cut into individual ribs.

5. Shave the corn kernels off the cobs and set aside. In a bowl, combine the mayonnaise, lime juice, sriracha, and cayenne pepper. Heat the oil in a wok over high heat. Add the corn kernels and constantly stir them to cook and get a good char, 7–10 minutes. Add the corn to the bowl and toss to coat.

6. Serve the ribs with the elote corn and pickled cucumbers.

Sunday Gravy

Dan

Rhode Island, and specifically the Providence area, has one of the highest populations of Italian Americans in the United States. Every Italian household, including mine, has their own version of gravy that they make on Sunday—but in this recipe, I use a pressure cooker to shorten that all-day cooking process to under an hour. I like to make my gravy using basil from my garden, and I even freeze basil that I grow at the end of each season, so we can use it throughout the cold New England winters. **Serves 8 to 10**

Meat and sauce

3 tablespoons olive oil, divided

1 small yellow onion, finely chopped

5 garlic cloves, sliced thin

4 bone-in country-style pork ribs

4 bone-in beef short ribs

Kosher salt and ground black pepper to taste

2 (28-ounce) cans whole San Marzano tomatoes

1 (6-ounce) can tomato paste

½ cup grated Pecorino Romano cheese, plus more for serving

3 cups water

½ cup dry red wine, such as Cabernet

1 tablespoon sugar

1 tablespoon onion powder

1 tablespoon granulated garlic

1 tablespoon dried parsley

2 tablespoons chopped fresh flat-leaf parsley

2 tablespoons chopped fresh basil

2 pounds pasta, such as penne, ziti, or small shells

Meatballs and sauce

2 cups Italian bread cubes

1 cup whole milk

4 tablespoons olive oil, divided, plus more as needed

1 shallot, minced

4 garlic cloves, minced

⅓ pound ground veal

⅓ pound ground pork

⅓ pound ground chuck

2 large eggs, lightly beaten

½ cup grated Pecorino Romano cheese

Kosher salt and ground black pepper to taste

½–¾ cup plain bread crumbs

1 (28-ounce) can whole San Marzano tomatoes

1 (6-ounce) can tomato paste

½ teaspoon onion powder

½ teaspoon granulated garlic

¼ teaspoon dried parsley

1. To make the meat sauce, set a pressure cooker to sauté. Heat 1 tablespoon of the olive oil, add the onion, and cook until lightly browned, about 5 minutes. Add the garlic and cook for 1 minute.

2. Meanwhile, heat 1 tablespoon of the olive oil in each of two large skillets over medium-high heat. Season the pork and beef ribs with salt and pepper and add them to the skillets. Cook until browned on both sides, 3–4 minutes per side.

3. Add the ribs to the pressure cooker, along with the tomatoes with their juices, tomato paste, Pecorino Romano cheese, water, wine, sugar, onion powder, granulated garlic, and dried parsley. Cover the pressure cooker, turn it to high pressure, and set the timer for 50 minutes.

4. When it is done, stir in the fresh parsley and basil. If there are any large pieces of tomato, break them up with a wooden spoon.

5. While the sauce is cooking in the pressure cooker, make the meatballs. Put the bread in a large bowl, add the milk, and set aside to soak.

6. Heat 2 tablespoons of the oil in a large skillet over low heat. Add the shallot and cook until slightly brown, about 5 minutes, then add the garlic and cook for 1 minute. Transfer to a bowl and set aside.

7. Add the meats, eggs, cheese, half of the sautéed shallot and garlic, and salt and pepper to the bowl with the bread and milk. Mix thoroughly, then add bread crumbs just until you can form meatballs that hold together. Form meatballs slightly larger than a golf ball in size.

8. Heat the remaining 2 tablespoons of oil in the same skillet over medium-high heat. Working in batches, cook the meatballs until browned on all sides, about 10 minutes. Transfer to a plate. Continue cooking, adding more oil as needed, until all the meatballs are cooked.

9. In a large pot, combine the tomatoes with their juices, tomato paste, and remaining sautéed shallot and garlic and cook for 3 minutes. Add the meatballs, onion powder, granulated garlic, dried parsley, and salt and pepper and bring to a boil. Reduce the heat and simmer for at least 20 minutes, or until the gravy is ready, stirring occasionally and breaking up the tomatoes with your spoon.

10. Bring a large pot of salted water to a boil and add the pasta. Cook until al dente according to the package instructions. Drain. Put the pasta in a large bowl and add enough sauce to coat. Ladle the pasta and sauce onto serving plates, and evenly divide the meat and meatballs on top. Top with grated Pecorino Romano cheese and serve.

Korean–Style Meatloaf and Potatoes

Tony

The Midwest is known for meat and potatoes, and when I was growing up, my family ate a lot of meatloaf. I remember never liking the flavor of the meatloaf or the ketchup glaze on top. Fast-forward years later, I faced my fears and made my own version of meatloaf, combining elements from Midwestern and Korean cultures. The classic loaf shape is upgraded with a super flavorful gochujang and ketchup sauce, making for a great fusion of cuisines. **Serves 6**

1 tablespoon unsalted butter

2 cups cubed slightly stale sourdough or white bread

½ cup whole milk

2 tablespoons vegetable oil

1 yellow onion, diced

6 garlic cloves, minced

2 tablespoons gochujang

8 ounces ground beef (80% lean)

8 ounces ground pork

8 ounces bacon, ground up or minced

2 large eggs, lightly beaten

⅔ cup chopped scallions, plus more for garnish

2 tablespoons toasted sesame oil

2 tablespoons soy sauce

1 teaspoon ground black pepper

Gochujang glaze

¼ cup gochujang

3 tablespoons ketchup

2 tablespoons hoisin sauce

2 tablespoons honey

2 tablespoons sugar

1 tablespoon rice wine vinegar

1 tablespoon soy sauce

1 teaspoon toasted sesame oil

2 garlic cloves, minced

Salt and ground black pepper to taste

3 tablespoons cold unsalted butter

Potatoes

4 tablespoons (½ stick) unsalted butter

3 tablespoons vegetable oil

5 large russet potatoes, peeled and diced small

1 large Vidalia onion, diced

3 garlic cloves, minced

1. Preheat the oven to 375 degrees F. Grease a 9 x 5-inch loaf pan with the butter.

2. In a large bowl, soak the bread cubes in the milk. Set aside.

3. In a medium skillet, heat the vegetable oil over medium-high heat. Add the onion and cook until translucent, 5–7 minutes. Near the end of that time, add the garlic and sauté for 1–2 minutes, or until fragrant. Add the gochujang and continue to cook and stir for another minute. Set aside to cool.

4. In another large bowl, combine the ground beef, pork, bacon, the soaked bread and any remaining liquid, eggs, scallions, sesame oil, soy sauce, pepper, and the cooled onion-garlic mixture. Mix thoroughly to combine. Pinch off a small portion and cook it in a small skillet for a couple of minutes, until fully cooked. Taste and make sure the mixture is seasoned appropriately. Once seasoned to your liking, transfer the mixture to the prepared loaf pan and pack it in evenly. Bake for 30 minutes.

5. While the meatloaf is baking, combine the gochujang, ketchup, hoisin, honey, sugar, rice wine vinegar, soy sauce, sesame oil, and garlic in a small saucepan. Whisk to combine and bring to a simmer over medium heat. Taste for seasoning and add salt and pepper. The sauce will thicken up after 7–10 minutes. Whisk in the cold butter, then remove the pan from the heat and set aside to cool.

6. When the meatloaf has been baking for 30 minutes, start brushing the top with the gochujang glaze every 3–4 minutes. Continue baking for another 10–15 minutes, or until the internal temperature reaches 140 degrees F. The sauce should caramelize on top; if needed, set the broiler on high for the last 5 minutes to help the sauce create a caramelized crust.

(recipe continues)

7. Meanwhile, make the potatoes. Heat the butter and oil in a large skillet over medium-high heat. Add the potatoes and cook for 10–15 minutes. Add the onion and garlic and continue to cook until the potatoes are golden-brown and fork-tender, 10–15 more minutes.

8. Slice the meatloaf and serve with a side of fried potatoes, topped with chopped scallions.

Pastelon

Sweet Plantain Lasagna

Irma

In the 1950s in New York City, a casserole dish could be a source of fusion and connection between the Puerto Rican and Italian communities. This dish highlights that fusion of cultures at its finest: pastelon mimics lasagna but is elevated with traditional flavors of Puerto Rico—an evolution that happened when the recipe was taken back and forth from New York to the islands and shared with loved ones who adapted it. Pastelon is a comforting dish cherished by all who come to discover it. **Serves 6**

Salted butter, for greasing

5–6 sweet ripe plantains

2 cups vegetable oil, for frying

2–4 tablespoons olive oil

1 cup sofrito

1 cup tomato sauce

¼ cup olive brine (from jarred olives), or to taste

1 teaspoon dried oregano

1 teaspoon ground coriander

1 teaspoon garlic powder

1 teaspoon onion powder

1 teaspoon ground annatto (achiote powder)

⅛ teaspoon ground turmeric

Salt and ground black pepper to taste

1½ pounds ground beef

2 cups shredded Mexican blend cheese

3 large eggs

---

1. Preheat the oven to 350 degrees F. Grease an 8 x 8-inch or 9 x 9-inch baking pan with butter.

2. Peel and slice your plantains: first, cut off both ends of each plantain. Then, with the tip of your knife, cut a shallow slice down the length of the plantain. Remove the peels by hand. Cut the plantains in half crosswise, then slice lengthwise into thin strips.

3. Heat the vegetable oil in a large skillet over medium heat. Fry the plantains until they are golden brown, turning them over halfway through, 5–6 minutes total. Set them aside on paper towels to drain. Wipe out the skillet.

4. In the same skillet, heat the olive oil over medium heat. Add the sofrito, allowing it to simmer about 1 minute or until aromatic, then add the tomato sauce, olive brine, oregano, coriander, garlic powder, onion powder, annatto, turmeric, salt, and pepper to the skillet and stir to combine. Taste and adjust seasoning as needed, then add the beef and cook over medium-high heat until the beef is browned. Again, taste and adjust seasoning. Remove the pan from the heat.

5. Make a layer of plantains in the prepared baking pan, top with some cheese, then add some of the ground beef and sauce. Repeat the layers until all the ingredients are used up, ending with a layer of cheese.

6. Whisk the eggs in a small bowl. Pour the eggs over the top of the pastelon; it will soak through as a binding agent. Bake for 35–40 minutes, or until golden and bubbly. Let cool for a bit, then slice and serve.

Albondigas in Chipotle Sauce with White Mexican Rice

Silvia

Spanish for meatballs and served in a broth, dry, or (as in this case) with a sauce, albondigas hold a special place in the hearts of many Mexicans. My grandma used to ask each of her grandchildren what their favorite dish was so she could make it for their birthdays. This is one I asked for often. Chipotle chiles are dried jalapeños. The most common way to buy them at the supermarket is canned in an adobo sauce, which gives them that classic smoky flavor. I added golden raisins at my husband's suggestion, and their sweetness balances beautifully with the acid, spice, and salt in the sauce. **Serves 4**

1 pound ground beef (85% lean)

1½ teaspoons salt, divided

¼ teaspoon ground black pepper

¼ teaspoon dried thyme

¼ teaspoon dried marjoram

2 medium eggs

¼ cup bread crumbs

¾ white onion, finely chopped

4 garlic cloves, minced

½ cup golden raisins

5 flat-leaf parsley sprigs, leaves picked and chopped, divided

1 pound Roma tomatoes

2 canned chipotle chiles in adobo sauce

1 cup chicken broth

1 tablespoon olive oil

8 (5- to 8-inch) corn tortillas, warmed

Rice

1½ cups white rice

1 tablespoon olive oil

¼ white onion, chopped

1 garlic clove, minced

3 cups water

1 tablespoon chicken bouillon powder

½ cup frozen peas

1 large carrot, peeled and chopped

Salt to taste

1. In a medium bowl, mix together the ground beef, 1 teaspoon of the salt, the pepper, thyme, marjoram, eggs, bread crumbs, half of the chopped onion, the garlic, golden raisins, and half of the chopped parsley. With your hands, form 12 meatballs. Set aside.

2. In a blender, blend the tomatoes, remaining chopped onion, chipotles, broth, and remaining ½ teaspoon salt until smooth.

3. Heat the oil in a medium saucepan over medium-high heat, pour in the sauce, and cook for 1 minute. Carefully submerge the meatballs in the sauce. Bring to a boil, then cover the pan, lower the temperature, and simmer for 25 minutes.

(recipe continues)

4. Meanwhile, rinse the rice until the water runs clear, then strain. Heat the oil in a small saucepan over high heat, then add the onion and garlic. Sauté until softened, about 5 minutes, then add the rice and sauté for 5 more minutes. Add the water and chicken bouillon and stir until dissolved. Add the frozen peas, carrot, and salt if needed. Cover the pan and bring to a boil. Turn the temperature down and simmer until the liquid evaporates and the rice is tender, 17–20 minutes.

5. Serve the albondigas with the rice and warm tortillas on the side. Garnish with the remaining chopped parsley.

Sizzlin' and Shakin' Beef with Coconut Jasmine Rice

Foo

This savory and sweet charred beef is rich with bold flavors and goes well with a steaming bowl of fluffy, lightly flavored coconut jasmine rice. This was the first dish I made for my wife when we just started dating. I wanted to impress her and express myself through my cooking, and I knew I could make this dish well. She liked it, and we still make it to this day! **Serves 4**

Pickled onion

¼ cup white vinegar

¼ cup rice vinegar

½ cup water

¼ cup sugar

½ teaspoon kosher salt

1 red onion, thinly sliced

Beef

1 tablespoon oyster sauce

1 tablespoon Maggi seasoning, soy sauce, or Worcestershire sauce

1 teaspoon dark soy sauce

2 tablespoons minced garlic

2 tablespoons finely chopped shallot

Salt and ground black pepper to taste

1 pound beef roast, cut into 1-inch chunks

1 red bell pepper, seeded and cut into strips

1 lime wedge

2 teaspoons toasted sesame seeds

Fried shallots, for garnish

Scallions, sliced, for garnish

Rice

2 cups jasmine rice

½ (13.5-ounce) can coconut milk

3 cups water

1 teaspoon salt

1 bay leaf

---

1. To make the pickled onion, combine the white vinegar, rice vinegar, water, sugar, and salt in a bowl and stir until the sugar and salt dissolve. Add the red onion and stir. Cover and refrigerate for 30 minutes.

2. Combine the oyster sauce, Maggi seasoning, dark soy sauce, garlic, shallot, and salt and pepper in a large bowl. Add the beef and toss to coat. Cover and refrigerate for 20 minutes.

3. Rinse the rice in a medium pot until the water is pretty clear; drain.

4. In a bowl, combine the coconut milk, water, salt, and bay leaf and mix well. Add the coconut milk mixture to the rice pot. Make sure that the rice is even and pour the liquid coconut mixture about 1½ inches above the rice. Cover the pot and bring to a boil over high heat. Uncover, reduce the heat to medium, and cook until all the liquid has been absorbed by the rice, about 20 minutes. Cover the pot again, reduce the heat to low, and cook for another 10 minutes, or until the rice is fluffy and fully cooked. Remove the bay leaf.

(recipe continues)

5. Heat a wok over high heat. Add the marinated beef and sauté, frequently stirring to evenly cook and char the beef, about 20 minutes. Remove the wok from the heat and stir in the bell pepper. Squeeze the lime wedge over the beef.

6. Scoop some rice into each bowl and ladle the beef over the rice. Garnish with sesame seeds, fried shallots, scallions, and pickled red onion and serve.

Korean Japchae Noodles

Tony

Whenever my brother and I get together, we love to have japchae noodles. A classic Korean dish of glass noodles, veggies, sesame, and soy sauce, this recipe is great as a side for a special occasion or even as a casual dinner. I make this recipe to celebrate Korean holidays and honor where I was born. I express love and care through my cooking, and when I make this dish I know that people can feel the love. **Serves 6**

½ cup soy sauce, divided

4 tablespoons toasted sesame oil, divided

4 tablespoons brown sugar, divided

2 teaspoons ground black pepper, divided, plus more to taste

6 garlic cloves, minced, divided

1 (8-ounce) boneless ribeye steak, sliced against the grain

4 cups spinach

4 tablespoons vegetable oil, divided

1 carrot, julienned

1 heaping cup sliced mushrooms (shiitake, brown, or white)

Salt to taste

½ Vidalia onion, thinly sliced

1 red bell pepper, seeded and julienned

1 jalapeño, julienned

6 scallions, quartered

1 (8-ounce) package sweet potato noodles (glass noodles)

3 large egg yolks, beaten

1 teaspoon sesame seeds

---

1. In a large bowl, whisk together ¼ cup of the soy sauce, 2 tablespoons of the sesame oil, 2 tablespoons of the brown sugar, 1 teaspoon of the black pepper, and 3 of the minced garlic cloves. Taste and add soy sauce or sugar if needed. Add the beef and toss to coat. Cover and marinate in the refrigerator for 30 minutes.

2. Bring a large pot of water to a boil. Fill a large bowl with cold water and ice cubes. Add the spinach to the boiling water and cook for 2–3 minutes. Using tongs, transfer the spinach to the ice bath (keep the water boiling for the noodles). Once cool, drain the spinach well, then divide among serving bowls.

3. Heat 2 tablespoons of the vegetable oil in a large skillet or wok over medium-high heat. Add the beef and cook until tender, 6–8 minutes. Transfer to a plate. Wipe out the skillet.

4. Heat the remaining 2 tablespoons vegetable oil in the same skillet over medium-high heat. Add the carrot and mushrooms, season with salt and pepper, and cook for 4 minutes. Add the onion, bell pepper, and jalapeño and cook for another 4 minutes. Add the scallions and cook for 2–3 minutes more. Set aside.

5. Add the noodles to the same pot of boiling water used for the spinach and cook according to the package directions.

6. While the noodles are cooking, in a small bowl, whisk together the remaining ¼ cup soy sauce, remaining 2 tablespoons sesame oil, remaining 2 tablespoons brown sugar, remaining 1 teaspoon black pepper, and remaining 3 minced garlic cloves. Set aside.

7. In a medium skillet, cook the egg yolks into a thin omelet. Remove from the heat and cut the omelet into ⅛-inch strips.

8. When the noodles are done, drain and transfer to a large bowl. Add the cooked veggies, beef, spinach, and omelet strips and mix until combined. Dress with the soy mixture and mix again. Taste for seasoning and adjust as needed. Top with sesame seeds and serve.

Beef Bulgogi with Quick Pickled Vegetables

Tony

This Korean beef is near and dear to me because my mom would make it every year for my "Arrival Day" (the day I first came to the US), alongside Mandu (pot stickers, page 13). I value my family very much, and I make this dish to show gratitude for our traditions and life together; whenever a friend wants to learn about Korean food, I use this dish as a stepping-stone to introduce them to the culture. The thinly sliced marinated beef cooks quickly and is delicious with the crisp and slightly spicy pickles. If you like, serve this dish with rice. **Serves 6**

---

1 cup soy sauce

6 tablespoons toasted sesame oil

¾ cup light brown sugar

1 Korean pear, peeled, cored, and pureed, *or* another ⅓ cup brown sugar

8 garlic cloves, minced

2 bunches scallions, 1 bunch chopped and 1 bunch quartered, plus 2 scallions, thinly sliced

1 tablespoon ground black pepper

3 pounds beef ribeye, thinly shaved

1 Vidalia onion, halved and sliced

6 tablespoons vegetable oil

2 heads romaine lettuce or 30 perilla leaves

2 teaspoons sesame seeds

2 carrots, peeled and julienned

Pickled vegetables

1 cup rice wine vinegar

1 cup water

1 tablespoon salt

1 tablespoon sugar

2 teaspoons gochugaru (Korean red pepper flakes)

2 English cucumbers, thinly sliced

1 Vidalia onion, thinly sliced

---

1. In a large bowl, whisk together the soy sauce, sesame oil, brown sugar, pear puree (if using), garlic, chopped scallions, and black pepper. Taste and add more salt or sugar if needed. Add the beef and onion and toss to coat. Cover and marinate in the refrigerator for at least 45 minutes and up to 2 hours.

2. Meanwhile, make the pickled vegetables. In a large bowl, whisk together the vinegar, water, salt, sugar, and gochugaru. Add the cucumbers and onion and toss to coat. Set aside to marinate in the refrigerator for at least 30 minutes.

3. When ready to cook the beef, heat 1–2 tablespoons of the vegetable oil in a large skillet or wok over medium-high heat (enough oil to cover the bottom). Working in batches so as to not crowd the pan, add some of the quartered scallions and some of the beef and fry just until the beef is cooked through, 5–7 minutes. Continue this process with more oil, scallions, and beef until it is all cooked.

(recipe continues)

4. Core the heads of romaine lettuce to access the smaller, crunchier leaves. Peel out enough of these leaves to have 4–5 on each plate.

5. Put some beef in the center of each plate. Add some of the pickled cucumbers and onion to the side, then garnish the beef and pickled vegetables with sesame seeds. Add some of the julienned carrots, lettuce leaves, and sliced scallions in a circle to surround the beef. Use the lettuce leaves to wrap up the meat and vegetables.

Back–to–School Fried Rice

Made with day-old rice, this is "everything in the fridge and pantry" fried rice, perfect to bring the family together on a fall evening after a busy work or school day. The saltiness of the canned meat balances the grilled sweet pineapples and sautéed shrimp. Pickled Chinese mustard greens bring another element of salt and acid. Complete with bright green peas and an "octo-dog," this is one whimsical dish you will truly enjoy. **Serves 6**

1 pineapple, peeled, cored, and cut into spears

4 tablespoons vegetable oil, divided

2 garlic cloves, minced

2 cups cooked jasmine rice, preferably cold

1 (12-ounce) can Spam, thinly sliced

¼ cup shrimp

Salt and ground black pepper

1 tablespoon fish sauce, plus a dash

2 large eggs

Garlic salt to taste

1 tablespoon soy sauce

1 cup fresh or frozen (thawed) peas

3 hot dogs

Fried onions, for garnish

Pickled mustard greens, for garnish

1. Preheat a grill. Grill the pineapple spears, then transfer to a cutting board and cut into ½-inch cubes. Set aside.

2. Heat 1 tablespoon of the oil in a wok over medium-high heat. Lightly sauté the garlic. Add the cooked rice and stir to coat. Remove the wok from the heat.

3. Heat another 1 tablespoon oil in a large skillet. Add the Spam and cook over medium-high heat until crispy. Transfer the Spam to a cutting board and dice; set aside.

4. Season the shrimp with salt, pepper, and a dash of fish sauce and add to the same skillet. Sauté over medium heat until fully cooked. Transfer the shrimp to a plate. Wipe out the skillet.

5. Whisk the eggs in a bowl and season with salt and pepper. Heat another 1 tablespoon oil in the same skillet over medium heat. Add the eggs and cook like an omelet. Transfer to a cutting board and cut into thin strips. Wipe out the skillet.

6. Add the Spam, shrimp, and omelet slices to the wok with the rice. Season with garlic salt, the soy sauce, and the remaining 1 tablespoon fish sauce. Add the pineapple and peas and cook for 3 minutes.

(recipe continues)

7. Cut the hot dogs in half crosswise. Make four even slits halfway up the cut end of each hot dog half.

8. Heat the remaining 1 tablespoon oil in the skillet over medium heat. Fry the hot dogs until the slits curl outward into an octopus shape.

9. Transfer the fried rice to serving bowls and top with fried onions and pickled mustard greens. Place an octopus hot dog on the rim of each bowl and serve.

Camarones Enchilados

Alejandra

Puerto Rican–Style Creole Shrimp

Camarones enchilados translates roughly to "deviled shrimp." The dish is not to be confused with Mexican enchiladas! The word *enchilado* refers to a dish that contains chiles (in this case, crushed red chile flakes). Gently simmered shrimp served in a flavorful tomato-based sauce is one of the very few spicy recipes in Puerto Rican cuisine. **Serves 4**

3 tablespoons olive oil

1 yellow onion, diced

2 red bell peppers, seeded and diced

4 large garlic cloves, minced

1 tablespoon smoked Spanish paprika

2 teaspoons ground cumin

1 teaspoon kosher salt,
   plus more to taste

½ teaspoon red pepper flakes,
   plus more to taste

½ cup dry red wine

1 (28-ounce) can crushed tomatoes

2 tablespoons capers

3 large bay leaves

2 pounds medium shrimp,
   peeled and deveined

1 tablespoon fresh lime juice,
   plus lime wedges for serving

¾ cup chopped fresh cilantro, plus
   more for garnish

Cooked white rice, for serving

1. Heat the oil in large, heavy-bottomed saucepan or Dutch oven over medium-high heat. Add the onion and bell peppers and cook, stirring occasionally, until they start to soften, about 5 minutes. Add the garlic, smoked paprika, cumin, salt, and red pepper flakes and cook until fragrant, 1–2 minutes.

2. Add the wine, tomatoes, capers, and bay leaves and bring to a boil. Reduce the heat and simmer, stirring occasionally, until the liquid is slightly thickened, 15–20 minutes.

3. Stir in the shrimp and cook just until opaque, about 3 minutes.

4. Remove from the heat and stir in the lime juice and cilantro. Taste and add more salt and red pepper flakes as needed. Remove and discard the bay leaves. Serve the shrimp and sauce over white rice, garnished with additional cilantro and lime wedges for squeezing.

Note: Shrimp cook quickly and are easy to overcook the longer they sit in the hot sauce. Be sure to be ready to serve immediately, or wait until just before serving to add the shrimp and finish the dish.

Beet, Fig, and Pine Nut Salad in Endive
(page 59) is also pictured

Fish in a Fig Leaf

Robin

The three most significant homes in my life—my childhood home, the home I bought for my children as a single mom, and my current home—have all had fig trees in the yard. Ancient wisdom held that if a fig tree did not bear fruit in three years, then it should be cut down. For me, the trees have come to signify the importance of making the most of your life and doing great things; if your life is not bearing fruit, then you are not living. This dish of salmon and fig sauce, cooked in fig leaves, combines two significant ingredients from my life's journey: figs, which are popular in the Mediterranean, and seafood, which is a big part of life on the Chesapeake Bay. They are prepared in a light and healthy way, the way I like to live and eat. **Serves 10**

Fig sauce

2 cups seedless red grapes

8 Mission figs, pitted

6 tablespoons unsalted butter, divided (see notes)

¼ cup fig balsamic vinegar

¼ cup honey

¼ teaspoon salt

¼ teaspoon red pepper flakes

2 rosemary sprigs

2 roasted garlic cloves (see notes)

Fish in a Fig Leaf

10 large (5-finger) fig leaves (see notes)

8 tablespoons olive oil, divided

10 (6-ounce) salmon fillets

Salt and ground black pepper to taste

2 purple yams, roasted and thinly sliced with a mandoline

2 zucchini, thinly sliced with a mandoline

2 yellow squash, thinly sliced with a mandoline

---

1. First, make the sauce. Puree the grapes and figs in a food processor and set aside. Melt 2 tablespoons of the butter in a small saucepan over medium heat. Whisk in the vinegar, honey, salt, red pepper flakes, and rosemary sprigs and stir as it thickens. Add the grape and fig puree, cover, and simmer for 8 minutes. Remove the rosemary and stir in the remaining 4 tablespoons butter and the roasted garlic. Set aside to cool while you prepare the fish.

2. Preheat the oven to 350 degrees F.

3. Lay out the fig leaves and brush one side of each fig leaf with olive oil.

4. Season the salmon fillets on both sides with salt.

5. Heat 2 tablespoons of the olive oil in a large skillet over medium heat. Working in batches, sear both sides of each salmon fillet quickly, just to get a little color, adding more oil to the pan as needed. Set one seared salmon fillet in the center of each fig leaf. Spread about 1½ tablespoons of the fig sauce on each salmon fillet. Lay a few slices of roasted yam on top. Fan out a few slices of the zucchini and yellow squash across the yam. Season with salt and pepper.

(recipe continues)

6. Wrap the fig leaves around the fish and vegetables and tie the bundles with cooking twine. Place the bundles in a large roasting pan. Bake for 12 minutes. Let rest for a few minutes before serving.

Notes: If you're making this dish alongside my Beet, Fig, and Pine Nut Salad in Endive (page 59), certain ingredients in these recipes serve double duty! The drippings from the pancetta in that recipe make a wonderfully salty, savory substitute for the butter in the fig sauce. Omit the butter and reserve 2 tablespoons of pancetta drippings. In the same pan the pancetta was cooked in, whisk the drippings with the vinegar, honey, spices, and rosemary, and proceed with the recipe as written. Reserve two of the roasted garlic cloves from the salad to use in the fig sauce. (Or, if you're serving this dish with other accompaniments, refer to that recipe for directions on roasting garlic.)

Fig leaves come in two sizes: 3-finger leaves and 5-finger leaves. You need 5-finger leaves to enclose the fish and veggies here—the smaller size wouldn't be big enough to wrap.

Pan–Seared Sea Bass in Tomato Sauce with Capers

Foo

My mother taught me how to prepare this dish, and I have been making it for a long time, adding my own takes to the recipe. The easy tomato sauce is made up of just six ingredients: tomatoes, garlic, shallots, capers, sugar, and fish sauce. (That's why the recipe is great to share—it is accessible for anyone at any level of culinary ability.) Vietnamese, Mexican, and Italian flavors all blend in this simple, nutritious dish that's perfect for a weekday dinner. **Serves 6**

---

1 tablespoon olive oil

2 tablespoons minced garlic

2 tablespoons minced shallot

4 Roma tomatoes, chopped

Salt and ground black pepper to taste

2 (28-ounce) cans whole San Marzano tomatoes

3 tablespoons fish sauce

2 tablespoons sugar

2 tablespoons capers

6 Chilean sea bass fillets

2 tablespoons vegetable oil

2 tablespoons chopped fresh cilantro

1 lemon, cut into wedges

---

1. Heat the olive oil in a large skillet over medium heat. Add the garlic and shallot and sauté just until translucent. Add the Roma tomatoes and salt and cook until the tomatoes are completely broken down, about 15 minutes.

2. Transfer the contents of the skillet to a blender and add the canned tomatoes with their juices. Blend until thick and smooth. Pour the tomato sauce back into the skillet and add the fish sauce, sugar, and capers. Cook over medium heat for 15 minutes.

3. Meanwhile, pat the sea bass fillets dry and season with salt and pepper. In another large skillet, heat the vegetable oil over medium heat and pan-sear the fillets for 8 minutes on each side.

4. Ladle some of the tomato sauce onto each plate. Place a fillet in the center of the plate and spoon a thin layer of tomato sauce over the fillet. Garnish with cilantro and squeeze a wedge of lemon over the fish.

Pasta with Pesto and Scallops

Nikki

For my fortieth birthday, I took a once-in-a-lifetime trip to Italy. One day after finishing a hiking trail, I stopped for something to eat in a small town, where the elders in the village served pesto and scallops. After returning home, I began re-creating the dish as an ode to them and to that trip, and my family now eats it regularly. The pesto and scallops are a perfect meeting of garden and sea and make for a quick and healthy weekday dinner option with an elegant flair. **Serves 4**

Pasta

1 pound linguine

Pesto

2 cups packed fresh basil leaves

2 garlic cloves, peeled

¼ cup toasted pine nuts

⅔ cup extra-virgin olive oil

1 teaspoon coarse sea salt

¼ teaspoon red pepper flakes

Grated zest and juice of 1 lemon

½ cup grated Parmesan cheese

Scallops

1 pound sea scallops

1 teaspoon coarse sea salt

Ground black pepper to taste

1 tablespoon vegetable oil

3 tablespoons grated Parmesan cheese

1. Bring a large pot of water to a boil. Add the linguine and cook according to the package instructions until al dente. Reserve ½ cup of the cooking water, then drain the pasta and return it to the pot; set aside.

2. Meanwhile, combine the basil, garlic, pine nuts, olive oil, a few tablespoons of reserved pasta cooking water, salt, red pepper flakes, lemon zest and juice, and Parmesan cheese in a blender or food processor and blend until smooth. Add more pasta cooking water as desired, blending after each addition, until the pesto reaches your desired consistency.

3. Pat the scallops dry with paper towels. Sprinkle the coarse sea salt and a grinding of pepper over the top.

4. Heat the vegetable oil in a large skillet (cast iron preferred) over medium heat. Add the scallops and sear until golden brown and opaque throughout, 75–90 seconds per side. Transfer the scallops to a plate.

5. Add the pesto to the linguine and toss to coat well. Using tongs, put some of the pesto pasta in each serving dish. Top with a few scallops and garnish with the Parmesan cheese.

Old School Mac 'n' Cheese for a Crowd

Tiffany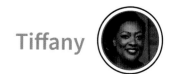

Mac 'n' cheese is a classic comfort dish that needs no introduction. This recipe makes enough to feed a big group! If you're serving for a smaller family, cut the amounts in half. **Serves 10–12**

1 pound elbow pasta

8 tablespoons (1 stick) unsalted butter

½ cup all-purpose flour

8 cups whole milk

2 tablespoons Dijon mustard

2 tablespoons Worcestershire sauce

1 tablespoon ground nutmeg

Salt and ground black pepper to taste

2 cups shredded sharp cheddar cheese

2 cups shredded mozzarella cheese

2 cups shredded pepper Jack cheese

1. Preheat the oven to 350 degrees F.

2. Bring a large pot of water to a boil. Add the pasta and cook according to the package directions until al dente. Drain.

3. Meanwhile, melt the butter in a medium pot over medium-high heat. Add the flour and stir with a wooden spoon until bubbly, about 3 minutes. Add the milk, mustard, Worcestershire, nutmeg, and salt and pepper and stir to combine.

4. Turn off the heat and stir in about three-quarters of the cheeses until melted.

5. Pour the pasta into a 13 x 9-inch size baking pan. Top with the remaining cheese. Cover the pan with aluminum foil and bake until the center is bubbly, about 30 minutes. Remove the foil and allow to brown for about 10 minutes. Serve immediately.

Holidays and
Special Occasions

Flank Steak with Italian Chimichurri

Nikki

and Roasted Parmesan Potatoes

I live in Boise, Idaho, where the grass-fed beef is exceptional and potatoes reign supreme. Every year, my husband and I get a quarter of a cow and we makes several steak dishes with the meat, including this tender flank steak drizzled with an herbaceous sauce. The chimichurri sauce and roasted Parmesan potatoes are nods to my Italian heritage and signature style of cooking. **Serves 4**

Steak and potatoes

1½ pounds flank steak

1 tablespoon coarse sea salt

½ teaspoon ground black pepper

3 red potatoes, diced

1 tablespoon olive oil

2 garlic cloves, sliced

1 teaspoon fine sea salt

¼ cup grated Parmesan cheese

Italian chimichurri sauce

1 bunch flat-leaf parsley, plus extra for garnish

½ bunch basil

1 tablespoon fresh oregano

6 garlic cloves, peeled

¾ cup olive oil

¼ cup red wine vinegar

½ teaspoon salt

1 teaspoon ground black pepper

½ teaspoon red pepper flakes

1 teaspoon grated lemon zest

1 tablespoon fresh lemon juice

1. Preheat the oven to 425 degrees F. Line a rimmed baking sheet with parchment paper.

2. Lay the flank steak out on another rimmed baking sheet. Sprinkle the coarse sea salt and pepper over the steak and let sit.

3. In a large bowl, toss the potatoes with the olive oil, sliced garlic, and fine sea salt until well coated. Spread the potatoes out on the lined baking sheet and roast for 25 minutes. Remove from the oven and sprinkle the Parmesan cheese over the potatoes. Return the potatoes to the oven and roast for another 8–12 minutes, or until the cheese is melted. Remove from the oven and set aside.

4. Combine all the chimichurri ingredients in a blender and pulse until combined but still chunky.

5. When the potatoes are nearly done, preheat the grill to medium-high. Grill the flank steak for 2 minutes on each side, or until an instant-read thermometer reaches 130 degrees F. Transfer to a cutting board and let rest for 5 minutes, then slice against the grain.

6. To serve, place some of the potatoes and steak on each plate and spoon chimichurri over the top of the steak.

Cast Iron Ribeye with Blue Cheese and Balsamic Steak Sauce

Brian

and Barbecue Brussels Sprouts

At my house, instead of eating meat and potatoes, we eat a lot of meat and sprouts. This hearty dinner pairs tender ribeye steak with herby blue cheese and a tangy steak sauce. The Brussels sprouts are sweet, funky, and loaded with bacon. This is not your usual weekday dinner! We're talking about bold and delicious flavors worthy of a special occasion—I guarantee you will love this dinner just as my family does. **Serves 4**

Sprouts

1 pound Brussels sprouts, quartered

8 thick slices bacon, cut into 1-inch pieces

2 tablespoons olive oil

¾ cup barbecue rub, such as B. T. Leigh's Somethin' for Rubbin', divided

Steak

8 tablespoons (1 stick) unsalted butter at room temperature

½ cup crumbled blue cheese

¼ teaspoon dried marjoram

1 (12-ounce) ribeye, at room temperature

⅔ cup steak seasoning, such as B. T. Leigh's Somethin' to Beef About

1 tablespoon grapeseed oil

Sauce

2 tablespoons chopped walnuts

1 tablespoon unsalted butter

¼ cup raisins

¼ cup apple cider vinegar

¼ cup water

1 tablespoon Worcestershire sauce

1 tablespoon tomato paste

1 teaspoon dried rosemary

1 tablespoon balsamic vinegar

1 tablespoon smoked salt

1. Preheat the oven to 400 degrees F and place a rimmed baking sheet in the oven to come to temperature.

2. Put the Brussels sprouts and bacon in a large bowl. Drizzle with the olive oil and toss to coat. Dust the sprouts with 2 tablespoons of the barbecue rub and toss again, coating evenly.

3. Pour the sprouts onto the preheated baking sheet and spread them out in a single layer, flat sides down to maximize surface contact for ultimate caramelization. The sprouts should sizzle when added to the pan.

4. Sprinkle the remaining spice rub over the top of the loaded baking sheet and return it to the oven. Roast for 20–30 minutes, scraping the pan and turning it halfway through the cooking time.

5. While the Brussels sprouts are roasting, make the steak. First, in a small bowl, combine the butter, blue cheese, and marjoram for the topping and set aside.

6. Pat the ribeye dry. Liberally coat it with the steak seasoning, pressing the rub into the beef. Let rest for at least 5 minutes.

7. Heat the grapeseed oil in a cast iron skillet over medium-high heat until it is smoking. Place the steak in the pan, tipping it toward you and pressing down gently to ensure good contact between the steak and the cast iron. Pan-fry the steak for 3 minutes, then flip, pressing it down again.

8. Add the butter topping to the steak and continue to fry until it reaches an internal temperature of 135 degrees F, about 3 minutes more. Place the steak on a wire rack to rest for 10 minutes.

(recipe continues)

9. While the steak rests, make the sauce. In a saucepan, toast the walnuts over medium heat. Add the butter and raisins and cook for 1 minute. Add the apple cider vinegar, water, Worcestershire sauce, tomato paste, and rosemary and cook until the tomato paste incorporates fully and begins to caramelize, about 5 minutes. Transfer the contents of the pan to a high-powered blender and blend on high until smooth, then strain the mixture through a double-mesh strainer back into the pot. Add the balsamic vinegar and smoked salt, stirring to combine over medium heat. Serve immediately or let cool.

10. Cut the ribeye against the grain into ¼-inch strips and fan out on the plate. Dollop the topping on the steak, then drizzle with the sauce, allowing the sauce to pool on one end of the plate next to the steak. Add the barbecue Brussels sprouts and serve.

 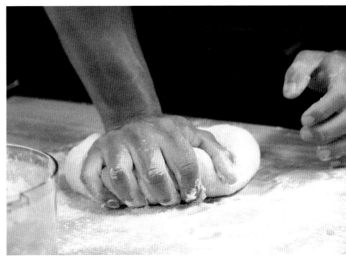

Beef and Beer Oyster Pie

Robin

This recipe celebrates my Maryland pride—with a twist. While my home state is known for its Chesapeake Bay oysters, having a British hubby introduced me to the British way of adding raw oysters to a hot beef pub pie. In these individual-sized pies, a savory beef and beer stew is baked with luscious puff pastry on top. **Serves 6**

2 pounds hanger steak, cut into bite-size pieces

Salt and ground black pepper to taste

4 tablespoons (½ stick) unsalted butter, divided

1 medium onion, chopped

Several rosemary, oregano, and thyme sprigs, tied together in a bundle

1 garlic clove, minced

1 tablespoon Dijon mustard

Pinch cayenne pepper

3 tablespoons all-purpose flour

1 tablespoon balsamic vinegar

1 (11-ounce) bottle Irish stout, such as Guinness, at room temperature

2 cups peeled chopped carrots

2 cups chopped button mushrooms

2 cups diced Yukon Gold potatoes

1 cup fresh or frozen (thawed) peas

1 (17.3-ounce) package frozen puff pastry, thawed

1 large egg

1 tablespoon water

2 tablespoons olive oil

1 tablespoon fresh lemon juice

1 shallot, minced

1 flat-leaf parsley sprig, minced

1 pint plump raw oysters in their shells

Lemon slices, for serving

1. Season the beef all over with salt and black pepper. Melt 1 tablespoon of the butter in a large skillet over medium heat. Add the onion and herb bundle and cook until the onion is caramelized and golden brown, about 5 minutes. Add the garlic, mustard, cayenne, and beef cubes and brown the beef on all sides.

2. Move the meat to the edges of the pan and add the remaining 3 tablespoons butter and the flour. Stir until the butter melts and blends with the flour. Stir in the balsamic vinegar. Mix the meat and onion together with the roux, stirring to coat the meat. Slowly pour in the stout and stir. Add the carrots, mushrooms, and potatoes. Reduce the heat to a low simmer. Cover and cook until the carrots and potatoes are fork-tender, about 20 minutes. Stir in the peas, turn off the heat, and remove the herb bundle.

3. While the stew is simmering, preheat the oven to 400 degrees F.

4. On a floured surface, roll out the puff pastry dough and cut out six rounds the same size as the bowls they will cover.

5. In a small bowl, whisk together the egg and water.

6. Divide the stew into six 8-ounce baking dishes that can also be used for serving. Place a pastry round on top of each bowl of stew, then brush with the egg wash. Cut a few slits in each pastry to allow steam to vent. Bake for about 20 minutes, or until the crust is golden.

7. In a small bowl, whisk together the olive oil, lemon juice, shallot, and parsley.

8. When the stew is ready to serve, place 2 oysters each on six small plates and nest a thin lemon slice alongside. Drizzle the lemon mixture across the tops of the oysters and add a pinch of salt. Each person should cut a hole in the top of their steaming-hot pie and slide the raw oysters into the hole so the oysters steam ever so slightly inside the pie.

Stuffed Veal Chops with Garlicky Spinach

Dan

My wife, Desiree, loves a good veal chop. We recently celebrated our thirtieth wedding anniversary—what a milestone event! For our dinner, I created this version of her favorite veal chop, stuffed with Italian cheeses and prosciutto. It's a wonderful meal to enjoy on your next special occasion. **Serves 6**

Stuffing

3 cups reduced-sodium chicken broth

4 tablespoons (½ stick) unsalted butter

1 (12-ounce) package herbed stuffing cubes

4 ounces fontina cheese, chopped

6 ounces buffalo mozzarella, chopped

½ cup grated Pecorino Romano cheese

8 slices prosciutto di Parma, chopped

Veal chops

6 (1-pound) milk-fed veal chops, frenched

Olive oil, for drizzling

½ teaspoon kosher salt

¼ teaspoon ground black pepper

Onion powder to taste

Granulated garlic to taste

Dried parsley to taste

Sauce

6 tablespoons cold unsalted butter

2 tablespoons minced shallot

¼ teaspoon all-purpose flour

1 cup dry red wine, such as pinot noir

4 cups reduced-sodium beef broth

6 tablespoons veal demi-glace

¼ teaspoon sugar

Spinach

¼ cup olive oil

8 garlic cloves, minced

½ teaspoon red pepper flakes

2 pounds baby spinach

½ teaspoon kosher salt

¼ teaspoon ground black pepper

1. Preheat the oven to 450 degrees F. Line a rimmed baking sheet with parchment paper and spray with nonstick cooking spray.

2. To make the stuffing, in a medium saucepan, bring the chicken broth and butter to a boil. Add the stuffing cubes, stir, and cover the pan. Turn off the heat. In a bowl, combine the fontina, mozzarella, Pecorino Romano, and prosciutto and mix well. Add the mixture to the stuffing and mix well. Cover.

3. Pat both side of the chops dry with paper towels. Cut a large slit in the side of each chop. Oil both sides of each chop and season with the salt, pepper, onion powder, granulated garlic, and dried parsley.

4. Fill each veal chop slit with stuffing and place the stuffed chops on the prepared baking sheet. Roast for 35–40 minutes, or until the internal temperature reaches 145 degrees F.

(recipe continues)

5. While the veal chops are roasting, make the sauce. Melt 2 tablespoons of the butter in a small saucepan over medium heat. Add the shallot and flour and cook until the shallot is softened. Add the wine and cook until reduced by half. Add the beef broth, demi-glace, and sugar and cook until reduced to about ¼ cup, 15–20 minutes. Strain the sauce and return it to the pan. Add the remaining 4 tablespoons butter, 1 tablespoon at a time, and whisk to incorporate.

6. To make the spinach, heat the olive oil in a large skillet over medium-low heat. Add the garlic and red pepper flakes and cook until the garlic is slightly browned. Add the spinach, salt, and pepper, cover the skillet, and turn the heat up to medium.

7. Cook just until the spinach is wilted, about 2–3 minutes.

8. Spoon some sauce onto each plate, lay a chop on the sauce, then add a little more sauce on top of the chop. Add some spinach on the side and serve.

Rack of Lamb and Mediterranean Orzo Salad with Haricots Verts

Robin

This is my favorite meal: tender, flavorful lamb chops with a briny orzo salad and sautéed haricots verts. No one can prepare it quite like my son Omar, who learned to cook from his Mediterranean grandma (I could not be prouder). It has become a tradition that he prepares this dish for me on my birthday, and it is the highlight meal of my year, every year. **Serves 4–6**

Lamb

2–3 racks of lamb, frenched (aim for 3 chops per person), trimmed of silverskin and excess fat

⅓ cup Dijon mustard

2 garlic cloves, minced

1 cup panko bread crumbs

1 tablespoon dried thyme

1 tablespoon dried oregano

Coarse salt to taste

1 bunch rosemary

Orzo

2 tablespoons unsalted butter

1 cup orzo

3 garlic cloves, minced, divided

1 teaspoon salt

2 cups boiling water

2 tablespoons olive oil

Juice of 1 lemon

⅓ cup sun-dried tomatoes, finely chopped

⅓ cup pitted kalamata olives, sliced

1 bunch fresh basil, leaves picked and chopped, plus a few sprigs for garnish

½ cup crumbled feta cheese

Haricots verts

1 pound haricots verts

1 shallot, chopped

Juice of 1 lemon

2 tablespoons olive oil

1 teaspoon dried oregano

½ teaspoon salt

1. Preheat the oven to 450 degrees F.

2. Place the lamb in a large roasting pan. Mix the mustard and garlic together and rub all over the lamb. Mix the panko and dried herbs together and rub all over the lamb. Season with coarse salt. Lay the rosemary sprigs between the chops.

3. Roast for 15–20 minutes, or until the lamb reaches an internal temperature of 120 degrees F. Let rest for 10 minutes.

4. Meanwhile, melt the butter in a medium saucepan over medium heat. Add the orzo and cook until slightly browned. Add 2 of the minced garlic cloves, the salt, and boiling water. Cook, stirring occasionally, until tender, about 12 minutes, then drain.

(recipe continues)

5. While the orzo is cooking, in a medium bowl, whisk together the olive oil, lemon juice, and remaining minced garlic clove.

6. Add the drained orzo to the bowl, toss gently, and season with salt as needed. Gently fold in the sun-dried tomatoes, olives, and basil. Set aside until ready to serve.

7. Combine the haricots verts, shallot, lemon juice, olive oil, oregano, and salt in a medium saucepan. Cover and cook over medium heat, stirring occasionally, until just tender, about 5 minutes. Keep an eye on them not to overcook and lose color.

8. Scoop some of the orzo in a mound in the center of each plate, then add 3 lamb chops on top of the orzo and some of the haricot verts to the side. Scatter the feta cheese over the plates. Garnish the lamb with a rosemary sprig and the orzo with a basil sprig.

Pernil
Puerto Rican Roasted Pork Shoulder

Alejandra

This marinated and slow-roasted pork shoulder is the star of many Puerto Rican holiday parties or family gatherings. But the features that make pernil such a perfect recipe for entertaining and celebrations also make it an ideal make-ahead dish for busy weekdays: you can prep and marinate the pork shoulder a couple of days ahead (or over the weekend) and let it slow-roast while you go about your day or prepare other dishes for your celebration. As with all traditional family recipes, there are many different versions of pernil, but this is the one I have made for my family for years. In my home we typically serve it with sides of rice and red beans, yuca with garlic mojo, and tostones. **Serves 8–10**

---

1 (5- to 8-pound) pork shoulder, bone-in with skin

1½ cups fresh Seville orange juice or tart grapefruit juice *or* equal parts lime juice and regular orange juice (see note)

¼ cup olive oil

2 tablespoons white vinegar

1 Spanish onion, quartered

16 large garlic cloves, peeled

1 large bunch cilantro, lower portion of stems removed

2 cubanelle peppers (Italian frying peppers) or green bell peppers, seeded

¼ cup smoked Spanish paprika

2 tablespoons ground cumin

2 tablespoons dried oregano

Kosher salt (1½ teaspoons per pound of pork)

2 teaspoons ground black pepper

---

1. Place the pork shoulder skin-side up in a large roasting pan. Use a paring knife to cut about 10 small, evenly spaced slits into the skin and fat.

2. Combine the orange juice, olive oil, vinegar, onion, garlic, cilantro, peppers, paprika, cumin, oregano, salt, and pepper in a blender or food processor and puree until smooth.

3. Pour the marinade all over the pork, rubbing it into any crevices and into the slits cut in the skin. Cover with plastic wrap and refrigerate for at least 6 hours and up to 2 days.

4. When ready to cook, preheat the oven to 325 degrees F with a rack in the lowest position.

5. Remove the pork from the refrigerator. Wipe off the excess marinade from the skin side, leaving any marinade that is still in the pan. Pour water into the pan so it goes 4 inches up the side of the pork. Cover the pan loosely with aluminum foil and roast for 6 hours, or until the meat is tender and pulls away easily with a fork.

6. Remove the foil, increase the oven temperature to 425 degrees F, and roast for another 1 hour, or until the skin is crisp. Serve warm.

Note: Seville oranges, known in Spanish as naranjas agrias, are a key ingredient in a lot of Puerto Rican and Cuban marinades. The tart oranges are closer to a lemon in flavor, but with a hint of floral sweetness that makes for an ideal ingredient in savory dishes. You can find them at Latin and Asian groceries, but if you can't, they can be replaced with either grapefruit juice or a mix of regular orange juice and lime juice.

Chiles en Nogada

Stuffed Poblano Peppers in Walnut Sauce

Silvia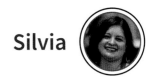

For those who've never had the pleasure, eating this classic Mexican dish is both a sweet and savory, soft and crunchy experience. The secret is in the balancing of all the elements. Stuffed Poblano Peppers in Walnut Sauce, known both in Mexico and abroad as chiles en nogada, honors the three colors of the Mexican flag. It is traditionally served around Mexican Independence Day in mid-September, although it can be served any time pomegranates are in season. **Serves 4**

---

6 poblano peppers

4 slices bacon, chopped

1 large white onion, chopped

2 garlic cloves, chopped

1 pound ground beef (85% lean)

4 ounces sliced deli ham, chopped

1 tart apple, such as Granny Smith, peeled, cored, and chopped

1 large peach, peeled, pitted, and chopped

¾ cup raisins

½ cup chopped roasted almonds

½ cup chopped pecans

2 bay leaves

1 tablespoon plus 2 teaspoons salt, divided

3 cups warm water

1 cup white vinegar

1 cup crema Mexicana (Mexican-style sour cream)

1 cup walnuts

4 ounces goat cheese

Pinch ground cinnamon

Seeds of 1 large pomegranate

1 bunch flat-leaf parsley, leaves picked and chopped

---

1. Roast the poblano peppers in a cast iron skillet or comal over medium-high heat, turning often, until blackened. Cover them with a kitchen towel and place them in a plastic bag. Let them sweat for 5–6 minutes, then remove the skins. Set aside.

2. Cook the bacon in a Dutch oven over medium-high heat until crispy. Add the onion and garlic, lower the heat to medium, and cook for 2 more minutes. Add the beef, ham, apple, peach, raisins, almonds, pecans, bay leaves, and 1½ teaspoons of the salt and mix well. Cover and let the filling cook for 30 minutes, stirring occasionally.

3. Slit each poblano pepper open from the stem down. Carefully open it and remove the seeds.

4. In a large bowl, mix the water, vinegar, and 1 tablespoon of the salt. Submerge the peppers and let them soak for 10 minutes, then drain and pat dry.

5. In a food processor, blend the crema Mexicana, walnuts, goat cheese, cinnamon, and remaining ½ teaspoon salt until smooth. The sauce has to be thin enough to cover the peppers easily, yet thick enough so you cannot see the green color under it. If it is too thick, add water, a teaspoon at a time, until you reach the desired consistency.

6. Fill the peppers with the meat mixture and place them on serving plates. Cover the peppers with the sauce and garnish with pomegranate seeds and parsley.

Grandma's Turkey Breast Stuffing

with Vegetables, Gravy, and Cranberry Compote

Robin

Mediterranean food was not the only food my mother passed down through the family. She made the best stuffing for the annual Thanksgiving turkey (although yes, she did add a wonderful Mediterranean twist to it, incorporating the roasted chestnuts of Italy into her amazing chestnut and sage stuffing). Now, I am the matriarch of my family, so I have taken liberties to make my mother's turkey and stuffing into what I call "Thanksgiving in a Bite." This dish has both dark and light meat and my stuffing all rolled up together. Served in slices, this turkey gives you all the flavors of dark and light meat and the stuffing in every bite. **Serves 6**

Turkey, stuffing, and gravy

1 (5-pound) boneless, skin-on turkey breast, trimmed and butterflied

Salt and ground black pepper to taste

1 large bunch sage, divided

6 tablespoons unsalted butter, divided

¼ cup olive oil

1 medium onion, chopped

4 celery stalks, chopped

1 pound ground dark turkey meat

2 hard bagels, finely chopped

½ cup roasted shelled chestnuts, chopped

2 tablespoons all-purpose flour

Vegetables

2 large sweet potatoes, peeled and cut into 1-inch cubes

3 tablespoons unsalted butter

1 large shallot, chopped

2 tablespoons apple cider vinegar

2 tablespoons sugar

1 slender red chile pepper, minced

8 ounces Brussels sprouts, cut in half

Salt and ground black pepper to taste

---

1. Preheat the oven to 400 degrees F.

2. Pound the turkey breast until it is mostly evenly thick throughout, then season both sides with salt and pepper. Taking care not to tear the skin, use your fingers to carefully separate the skin from the meat and slide a few sage sprigs under the skin.

3. Heat 2 tablespoons of the butter and the oil in a large cast iron skillet over medium-high heat. Add the turkey, skin-side down, and sear it, then turn it over and sear the underside.

4. Transfer the turkey, skin-side down, to a large sheet of parchment paper and set aside.

5. Chop 10 large sage leaves.

(recipe continues)

6. In the same skillet, heat another 2 tablespoons butter over medium heat. Add the onion, celery, sage, and ground dark turkey and cook, stirring to break up the meat, until no longer pink, about 10 minutes. Add the chopped bagels and chestnuts and continue cooking just until heated through.

7. Remove the stuffing from the pan, reserving the pan with its juices for the gravy, and place the stuffing on top of the breast. Roll the breast up as tightly as possible and tie in several places with kitchen twine. Transfer to a roasting pan, cover with aluminum foil, and bake for 30 minutes. Remove the foil and continue roasting for about 25 minutes more, or until an instant-read thermometer registers 155 degrees F.

8. Remove the turkey from the oven and let it rest for 10 minutes. The internal temperature should rise to 165 degrees F. Transfer the turkey to a cutting board. Pour a few spoonfuls of boiling water into the roasting pan and set aside.

9. Bring a medium pot of salted water to a boil. Add the sweet potatoes and cook for 2 minutes.

10. Melt the butter in a large skillet over medium heat. Add the shallot, vinegar, sugar, chile pepper, and sprouts. Using a slotted spoon, remove the potatoes from the boiling water and add them to the skillet.

11. Season with salt and pepper and cook just until tender, about 10 minutes. Remove from the heat.

12. To make the gravy, place the skillet used to make the stuffing over medium heat. Add the remaining 2 tablespoons butter and the flour and stir until it forms a roux (paste). Pour the watered-down liquid from the turkey roasting pan into the roux and whisk until it thickens into a gravy. Season with salt and pepper.

13. Carve the stuffed turkey into thick slices, removing the twine as you go. Place two or three slices on each plate, top with the gravy, and add a spoonful of sweet potatoes and Brussels sprouts. Serve with cranberry compote on the side.

Cranberry Compote

12 ounces fresh cranberries	2 tablespoons sugar
12 ounces seedless red grapes	1 tablespoon unsalted butter, at room temperature
1 shallot, peeled	¼ teaspoon red pepper flakes
2 tablespoons balsamic vinegar	¼ cup marsala wine

1. Combine all the compote ingredients in a food processor and puree. Transfer to a medium saucepan and bring to a simmer, then turn the heat down to low, cover, and cook for 15 minutes.

Planked Molasses Salmon

Nikki

My husband made this dish on our very first date, so you know it will impress your guests or family on a special evening! Light salmon is coated with a molasses glaze to make a dish that beautifully blends contrasting flavors: sweet and savory, smoky and fresh. This dish will exceed your expectations and surprise you. **Serves 4**

---

4 zucchinis, sliced lengthwise

2 tablespoons olive oil, divided

2 pinches sea salt

1½ pounds king salmon fillets

3 tablespoons molasses

2 tablespoons brown sugar

2 garlic cloves, minced

2 lemons, 1 thinly sliced and 1 cut into wedges

---

1. Soak a large cedar plank in water for at least 30 minutes (see note). Drain and pat dry. Line a baking sheet with foil.

2. Preheat the oven to 525 degrees F or high broil with a rack in the lowest position.

3. Put the zucchini slices in a large bowl. Add 1 tablespoon of the olive oil and a pinch of salt and toss well. Let sit while you prepare the salmon.

4. Place the salmon on the plank and set the plank on the prepared baking sheet.

5. In a small bowl, mix the remaining 1 tablespoon olive oil, molasses, brown sugar, garlic, and a pinch of salt and combine well. Smear the mixture over the top of the salmon fillets. Place the lemon slices on top of the molasses mixture.

6. Roast the salmon on the lowest rack for 8–10 minutes, or until the center of the salmon flakes easily with a fork. Remove from the oven and let rest while you make the zucchini.

7. Place the zucchini on a grill pan over medium-high heat and sear for 2–3 minutes on each side.

8. Serve the salmon with the zucchini, garnished with lemon wedges.

Note: Instead of using a cedar plank, you can roast the salmon fillets on a rimmed baking sheet lined with aluminum foil.

Italian Baccala

Nikki

My family loves to share this tomato and vegetable-based stew with salted cod every Christmas Eve as part of the Feast of the Seven Fishes. It is warm and hearty—a bowl of love—and the meal itself is a gift to our guests! The cod has a pleasantly firm, flaky texture and a savory flavor. This holiday dish has been maintained by each generation that makes it, representing hundreds of years of our Italian tradition. My family brought this recipe to the United States when they emigrated from Italy, and getting to make it at the holidays was a rite of passage for me. **Serves 8**

1½ pounds salted cod (baccala)

1 eggplant, peeled and diced

Coarse sea salt as needed

3 tablespoons olive oil, divided, plus more for drizzling

1 yellow onion, diced

2 carrots, peeled and sliced

2 celery stalks, sliced

2 cups long-stem green beans, trimmed and halved

2 red bell peppers, seeded and diced

1 yellow bell pepper, seeded and diced

2 zucchini, sliced

8 garlic cloves, sliced

1 (28-ounce) can crushed San Marzano tomatoes

1 (28-ounce) can petite diced San Marzano tomatoes

2 tablespoons chopped fresh basil

2 tablespoons dried Italian seasoning

2 tablespoons dried parsley

2 tablespoons dried oregano

2 tablespoons garlic powder

2 teaspoons ground black pepper

2 teaspoons red pepper flakes

2 cups dry red wine, such as burgundy or chianti

Crusty Italian baguette

½ cup grated aged Parmigiano-Reggiano cheese

---

1. Soak the salted cod in cold water for 24 hours, then drain and rinse well. Pat dry and cut into ½-inch chunks (I cut this small so the kids don't know they're eating fish).

2. Put the eggplant in a colander, sprinkle with coarse salt, and place something heavy on top (like a couple of cans of tomatoes). Let the eggplant sweat in the sink for 2 hours. Rinse and pat dry.

3. In a large skillet over medium heat, sauté each vegetable individually (onion, carrots, celery, green beans, bell peppers, zucchini, and eggplant) with some of the oil, garlic, and seasonings until al dente, 3–5 minutes. As each vegetable is done, transfer it to a large pot. Turn the heat under the pot to medium-low. Add the cans of tomatoes with their juices to the pot along with a large pinch of salt and mix well. Add the remaining basil, Italian seasoning, parsley, oregano, garlic powder, black pepper, and red pepper flakes, stir well, and bring to a simmer.

4. Add the cod and wine to the pot, cover, and cook for 25–30 minutes. Taste and add more salt or pepper if needed.

5. Preheat the oven to 375 degrees F.

6. Place the baguette directly on the oven rack and let warm for 7–9 minutes. Remove from the oven and slice.

7. Ladle the baccala into big soup bowls. Garnish with the grated cheese, drizzle with olive oil, and serve bread on the side for soaking up the broth.

Gnocchi and Buffalo Mozzarella

Dan

Making gnocchi from scratch is a tradition that is not practiced very much these days. It is so worth the time and effort, though—and it really isn't as hard as it seems. This dish holds a lot of nostalgia for me because all the "old-timers" in my family used to make it. When I bring this dish to family gatherings, it prompts discussions about our family's history and reminds us of all of the joy we have experienced in the kitchen together. **Serves 6**

Gnocchi

8 small Idaho potatoes

1 large egg

¾ cup grated Parmigiano-Reggiano cheese

½ teaspoon olive oil

1½ teaspoons salt

1½–2 cups all-purpose flour

Sauce

2 tablespoons olive oil

1 tablespoon minced shallot

2 garlic cloves, thinly sliced

1 (28-ounce) can whole San Marzano tomatoes

¼ cup plus 1 tablespoon grated Pecorino Romano cheese

½ teaspoon onion powder

½ teaspoon granulated garlic

¼ teaspoon dried parsley

Kosher salt and ground black pepper to taste

1 tablespoon cold unsalted butter

2 tablespoons chopped fresh flat-leaf parsley, divided

2 tablespoons chopped fresh basil, divided

1 large (25-ounce) ball buffalo mozzarella, cubed

---

1. Line a rimmed baking sheet with parchment paper and put it in the freezer. Put the potatoes on a microwave-safe plate and microwave until they are fork-tender, about 12 minutes. While the potatoes are still hot, peel them and pass them through a food mill or ricer onto the cold parchment-lined baking sheet. Try to keep the potatoes as light and fluffy as possible. Refrigerate the potatoes on the baking sheet until cold.

2. Transfer the cold potatoes to a clean work surface. In a bowl, beat together the egg, Parmigiano-Reggiano, oil, and salt and pour the mixture over the potatoes. Cover generously with 1½ cups of the flour. It should look like snow on the mountains.

3. Crumble the potato-flour mixture between your fingers, then begin to knead the dough until it is a dry, homogeneous mixture. The dough should feel slightly moist, but not tacky. If too tacky, repeat the "snow on the mountains" stage with some of the remaining ½ cup flour. Flatten the dough into a disk, wrap it in plastic wrap, and let rest in the refrigerator for 30 minutes.

4. While the dough is resting, make the sauce. Heat the oil in a large skillet over medium-low heat. Add the shallot and garlic and cook until soft, 4–5 minutes. Add the tomatoes with their juices, ¼ cup of the Pecorino Romano, the onion powder, granulated garlic, dried parsley, salt, and pepper. Turn the heat up to medium and simmer the sauce for 25 minutes, stirring occasionally and breaking up the tomatoes with a spoon. Turn off the heat and add the butter and 1 tablespoon each fresh parsley and basil.

5. Dust a rimmed baking sheet with flour. Form the dough into a large log. Cut slices off the log and begin to roll them into long ropes that are about 1 inch thick. Cut the ropes into ½-inch lengths. Cover generously with flour. Place the gnocchi in a single layer on the floured baking sheet.

6. Bring a large pot of salted water to a boil. Fill a large bowl with cold water. Working in batches, add the gnocchi and cook until they puff up and float to the surface, about 4 minutes. Taste one to make sure they are done. Using a slotted spoon, transfer to the cold water for 2 minutes, then drain.

7. Turn the heat under the sauce to medium. Add the gnocchi to the sauce, along with the mozzarella. Cook for 2 minutes, tossing lightly, then transfer to a serving dish. Garnish with the remaining 1 tablespoon each fresh parsley, basil, and Pecorino Romano.

Brunch

Chicken and Waffle Sandwiches and Fruit Kabobs
with a Watermelon Cocktail or Mocktail 184

LOU to NSH: Biscuit Trio 187

Red Chilaquiles 193

Shakshuka with Chive Flatbread 194

Tortilla Española 196
(Spanish Potato Omelet)

Potato Crust Herb Quiche 198

Maple Pumpkin Bread 201

Chicken and Waffle Sandwiches and Fruit Kabobs

Robin

with a Watermelon Cocktail or Mocktail

Picnic and boating season in Maryland happens to arrive as watermelons and mint are ripe for picking. And with more than two thousand poultry farms throughout Maryland, well, these ingredients just go together naturally. When I found a kindred spirit who loves to cook for everyone as much as I do, we spent a weekend together and did just that—cooked! She showed me how to make the Southern classic chicken and waffles. Inspired to turn the dish into sandwiches, we packed them for a picnic, which we took on a hike to a one-hundred-year-old barn. At the end, we sat on bales of hay and enjoyed their crisp, sweet, spicy deliciousness wrapped and tied in easy-to-transport bundles. These chicken and waffle sandwiches with a spicy honey drizzle make an excellent summertime brunch or picnic lunch—especially with a watermelon cocktail to wash them down. **Serves 6**

Chicken

1 cup buttermilk

2 garlic cloves, gently smashed

6 boneless, skinless chicken thighs, cut in half through the width to make thinner pieces

2 cups all-purpose flour

2 tablespoons cornstarch

1 teaspoon baking powder

2 teaspoons chili powder

Salt to taste

2 tablespoons vegetable oil, or more as needed

⅓ cup honey

½ teaspoon red pepper flakes

3 large tomatoes, sliced

1 large bunch basil, leaves picked

Waffles

3 large eggs, separated

3 cups whole milk

3 tablespoons sugar

1 stick (8 tablespoons) unsalted butter, melted and slightly cooled

3 cups all-purpose flour

1 tablespoon baking powder

1 teaspoon salt

½ teaspoon ground cinnamon

1 bunch chives, finely chopped

Fruit kabobs

1 bunch green grapes

1 pint blackberries

1 pint raspberries

---

1. Preheat the oven to 350 degrees F. Line a rimmed baking sheet with parchment paper.

2. Put the buttermilk and garlic in a large bowl. Add the chicken thighs and let soak.

3. In another large bowl, combine the flour, cornstarch, baking powder, chili powder, and salt.

4. Heat the oil in a large skillet over medium-high heat.

5. One by one, remove each piece of chicken from the milk and let the excess drip back into the bowl. Dip the chicken in the flour mixture, shake off the excess, and place in the skillet, adding only as many pieces as you can without crowding. Brown the chicken quickly on both sides, then transfer to the lined baking sheet. Continue with all the pieces, adding more oil if needed.

6. Place the baking sheet in the oven and bake for about 20 minutes, or until the chicken is cooked through.

7. Meanwhile, heat a waffle iron.

8. In a small bowl, whip the egg whites using a hand mixer.

9. In a large bowl, whisk together the milk, sugar, and egg yolks, then slowly whisk in the melted butter. Whisk in the flour, baking powder, salt, and cinnamon. Fold in the egg whites.

(recipe continues)

10. Make the waffles according to the manufacturer's instructions, and lay them on parchment paper when done.

11. While the waffles cook, put the grapes and berries on kabob sticks. If you are packing your meal to go, wrap parchment paper around each stick, leaving just the top berry exposed.

12. In a small bowl, whisk together the honey and red pepper flakes. As soon as the chicken is out of the oven, drizzle the chili honey across all the chicken pieces while they cool.

13. If you're packing your sandwiches to go, cut sheets of parchment paper in half to use as wrappers for each sandwich; if you're serving right away, you can skip wrapping them. Set one waffle on each paper, then one chicken thigh, then a thin slice of tomato and a sprinkle of salt and pepper, and a large basil leaf. Fold the waffle to make a sandwich or place another waffle on top. Sprinkle with chives for a bit of color. Wrap the paper around the sandwich, leaving the top third of the sandwich exposed. Tie kitchen twine around the wrappers.

14. Place the sandwiches in a small napkin-lined basket along with the fruit kabobs sticking out.

Watermelon Cocktail or Mocktail

4 cups cold watermelon chunks

Juice of 2 limes

2 tablespoons sugar

6 watermelon wedges with rind, about 2 x 1 inch, for garnish

6 large mint leaves

1¼ cups vodka (optional)

Ice cubes

12 ounces chilled sparkling water, or more for mocktails

1. Puree the watermelon chunks in a blender or food processor. Strain the puree through a fine-mesh sieve and reserve 2½–3 cups of juice; refrigerate until ready to serve.

2. In a small saucepan, combine the lime juice and sugar and simmer just until the sugar dissolves. Set aside to cool a bit, then whisk the syrup into the chilled watermelon juice.

3. For each drink, thread one watermelon wedge and one mint leaf on a 4-inch kabob stick to lay across the glass as a garnish.

4. Pour 2 ounces watermelon juice and 1½ ounces vodka (if using) into each chilled glass, add ice and chilled sparkling water, and serve.

LOU to NSH: Biscuit Trio

Brian

There's nothing more iconic in my neck of the woods than biscuits. Add some fried chicken and a cheese sauce and you've got heaven. This trio of biscuit sandwiches takes you on a road trip down I-65 from Louisville to Nashville—from hot brown to pimento cheese to Nashville hot chicken, this is the South on a plate.
Serves 4 (3 biscuits per serving)

Pimento cheese

4 ounces smoked Gouda cheese, shredded

4 ounces extra sharp cheddar cheese, shredded

4 ounces cream cheese, softened

2 tablespoons mayonnaise

1 tablespoon Dijon mustard

2 tablespoons chopped pickled jalapeños

2 tablespoons chopped pimentos

2 tablespoons sweet relish

Kentucky bar fight sauce

¼ cup blackberries

¼ cup blueberries

½ jalapeño, diced

1½ teaspoons white sugar

1 tablespoon strong brewed coffee

1 tablespoon bourbon

1½ teaspoons cornstarch

Hot chicken

Peanut oil, for deep frying

2 cups all-purpose flour, divided

2 teaspoons kosher salt plus a pinch, divided

1 teaspoon ground black pepper

1 large egg

1 tablespoon cayenne pepper

1 tablespoon garlic powder

4 boneless, skin-on chicken thighs

Dill pickle slices, for garnish

Hot dip

2 tablespoons dark brown sugar

1 tablespoon cayenne pepper

1 teaspoon Scotch Bonnet flakes

1 teaspoon garlic powder

1 teaspoon smoked paprika

1 teaspoon ground sumac

Biscuits

12 tablespoons (1½ sticks) cold unsalted European-style butter, such as Plugra

3 cups all-purpose flour, plus more for dusting

1½ tablespoons baking powder

1½ tablespoons white sugar

1½ teaspoons kosher salt

2 cups buttermilk

3 tablespoons melted butter, for brushing

Finishing salt, such as Maldon, for sprinkling

Hot brown

6 slices bacon, cut in half crosswise

4 boneless, skin-on chicken thighs

1½ teaspoons citrus herb rub, such as B. T. Leigh's Somethin' to Cluck About, plus more for garnish

½ teaspoon kosher salt

½ tomato, sliced thin

Mornay sauce

1 tablespoon unsalted butter

1 tablespoon all-purpose flour

1 cup whole milk

½ teaspoon onion powder

½ teaspoon kosher salt

¼ cup shredded Gruyère cheese

1 tablespoon grated Parmesan cheese

(recipe continues)

1. To make the pimento cheese, combine the shredded Gouda and cheddar cheeses, cream cheese, mayonnaise, mustard, pickled jalapeños, pimentos, and sweet relish in a food processor. Pulse until the mixture comes together; it should still be chunky. Cover and refrigerate until ready to serve.

2. To make the Kentucky bar fight sauce, combine the blackberries, blueberries, and jalapeño in a saucepan over medium heat. Using a potato masher, crush the berries. They will begin to release their liquid as they soften. Cook the berries until all the juices are released, about 5 minutes. Transfer the mixture to a fine-mesh strainer and strain the mixture into a bowl; discard the solids in the strainer. Return the mixture to the saucepan and add the white sugar. Bring to a boil.

3. In a small bowl, whisk together the coffee, bourbon, and cornstarch until smooth. Add the mixture to the saucepan, whisking continuously until it reaches a boil and the sauce is thickened, about 5 minutes. Remove from the heat and set aside to let cool.

4. To make the hot chicken, pour the peanut oil into a Dutch oven and heat to 325 degrees F.

5. Set up your coating station with three shallow bowls. In the first bowl, whisk together 1 cup of the flour, 1 teaspoon of the salt, and the black pepper. In the second bowl, beat the egg and a pinch of salt. In the third bowl, whisk together the remaining 1 cup flour, remaining 1 teaspoon salt, cayenne pepper, and garlic powder.

6. Set a wire rack on top of a baking sheet. Pat the chicken dry with paper towels. First, coat the chicken thighs in the bowl with flour, salt, and black pepper; shake off the excess. Next, dip the chicken thighs in the egg mixture; shake off the excess. Finally, dip the chicken thighs in the bowl with the flour and seasonings; shake off the excess. Place the thighs on the prepared rack and let them sit for at least 10 minutes before frying.

7. When ready to fry, carefully lower the chicken into the hot oil. Fry until deep golden brown, using a spider or large slotted spoon to turn the chicken over occasionally. It should take 7–8 minutes per side. Meanwhile, set a clean rack on top of a clean baking sheet. Transfer the cooked chicken to the rack. Check the internal temperature, making sure the chicken is cooked to 165 degrees F. Do not discard the oil yet.

8. While the chicken is resting, make the hot dip. In a large bowl, combine the brown sugar, cayenne pepper, Scotch Bonnet flakes, garlic powder, smoked paprika, and sumac. Slowly and very carefully, whisk in 1 cup of the peanut oil left over from frying.

9. Using a spider or slotted spoon, dip the chicken in the spiced oil and set back on the rack.

10. To make the biscuits, preheat the oven to 425 degrees F. Line a rimmed baking sheet with parchment paper.

11. Using the small holes of a box grater, grate the cold butter into a large cold bowl. The finer the butter, the better. Place the butter and bowl in the freezer.

(recipe continues)

12. In a second large bowl, whisk together the flour, baking powder, white sugar, and salt.

13. Once the oven is preheated completely, remove the butter from the freezer and cut it into the flour mixture using a pastry cutter (a bench scraper or your fingertips will work too) until the mixture looks like crumbs. There should be some pea-size lumps of butter remaining. Add the buttermilk and stir until combined. The dough should be wet and sticky.

14. Transfer the dough to a well-floured work surface. Dust the top of the dough with flour as well. Gently work the dough until it comes together, then fold it in half using a bench scraper and gently flatten with the palm of your hand. Repeat this kneading process five more times, folding the dough in on itself each time.

15. Using your hands, flatten the dough to about 1 inch thick and cut out biscuits with a 2¾-inch biscuit cutter, pressing straight down rather than twisting the cutter. Dip the cutter in flour before each use to keep the dough from sticking to it. Cut as many biscuits as possible.

16. Place the biscuits on the lined baking sheet with the biscuits just touching each other, in rows of four. Lightly press your thumb into the middle of each biscuit to keep the tops from doming.

17. Rework the remaining dough and repeat the process until you have as many biscuits as you can; you should end up with 12–14 total.

18. Bake for 15–20 minutes. At 15 minutes, start checking the biscuits: the bottoms should be a light golden brown. Once the bottom is perfect, turn on the broiler and brown the tops of the biscuits for 1 minute, or until nicely colored.

19. Remove the biscuits from the oven. Brush with the melted butter and sprinkle with finishing salt. Serve hot.

20. To make the hot brown, in a large skillet, cook the bacon over medium heat.

21. While the bacon is cooking, trim the chicken thighs to be the approximate size of the biscuits. Season the chicken thighs with the citrus herb rub and salt.

22. Transfer the bacon to paper towels to drain.

23. Add the chicken thighs to the bacon fat remaining in the skillet and fry the chicken, turning once. Once they are golden brown and have reached an internal temperature of 165 degrees F, about 15 minutes, then transfer to a plate.

24. To make the Mornay sauce, melt the butter in a small saucepan over medium-high heat until it is foaming. Add the flour and whisk to form a paste. Let the paste cook until it is slightly blond in color and there is no longer a raw flour smell. Begin to slowly add the milk, whisking constantly. The mixture will clump, become smooth, and finally begin to thicken. Add the onion powder and salt. Continue to whisk.

25. Once the sauce begins to thicken, reduce the heat to low and slowly begin incorporating the Gruyère. Add a small amount of cheese, whisk until incorporated, and then add another small amount of cheese. Continue until all the Gruyère is incorporated and the sauce is smooth.

26. Repeat the same process with the Parmesan cheese.

27. Set the sauce aside, off the heat. If it gets too cold, heat gently over a low burner.

28. To plate each serving, using a fork, split three biscuits. Place the bottoms of the biscuits on a plate. Set the tops of the biscuits to the side.

29. On one biscuit, place a hot fried chicken thigh, then spoon some of the hot dip over the chicken. Top with a few dill pickle slices.

30. On the second biscuit, place a dollop of pimento cheese, then drizzle with some of the bar fight sauce.

31. On the last biscuit, place a pan-fried chicken thigh, add a tomato slice on top of the chicken thigh, then 2 bacon slices on the tomato, and finally a spoonful of the Mornay sauce. Dust with a pinch of citrus herb rub.

32. Place the biscuit tops on each sandwich and serve immediately.

Red Chilaquiles

Silvia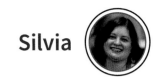

A popular Mexican breakfast, red chilaquiles are made with tortillas, salsa, cheese, and eggs or meat. I grew up eating this dish and find it comforting. Every Mexican family has their signature way of making chilaquiles. Some people fry the tortillas and simmer them in the salsa, creating a soft consistency. I like to add different textures to my dishes, so I prefer crunchy tortillas layered with homemade salsa and topped with sunny-side-up eggs. Buen provecho! **Serves 4**

Vegetable oil, for frying

16 (6- or 8-inch) corn tortillas, cut into triangles

1 teaspoon salt, plus more to season tortillas

1 pound tomatoes

2 jalapeños

½ white onion

2 small garlic cloves, peeled

1½ tablespoons dried Mexican oregano

4–5 tablespoons water

4 large eggs

Ground black pepper to taste

10 ounces queso fresco, crumbled

1 large avocado, peeled, pitted, and sliced

1 small bunch cilantro, leaves picked and chopped, for garnish

---

1. Pour the oil into a deep fryer or large, heavy-bottomed pot and heat to 350 degrees F. Working in batches, fry the tortilla triangles until golden brown. Transfer to paper towels and sprinkle with a little salt. Set aside.

2. In a cast iron skillet or comal, roast the tomatoes, jalapeños, onion, and garlic over medium-high heat, turning often, until soft, 10–12 minutes.

3. Remove the jalapeño stems and put all the vegetables in a blender. Add the oregano, salt, and 4–5 tablespoons of water (depending on how liquidy you like the salsa). Blend until smooth. Pour the salsa into a saucepan and cover to keep it warm.

4. Add enough oil to cover the surface of a nonstick skillet and cook the eggs sunny-side up. Season them with salt and pepper.

5. Pour a little bit of salsa on each plate, add a layer of fried tortillas, and then add more salsa. Place an egg on top, add more salsa, and finish with crumbled queso fresco, sliced avocado, and chopped cilantro.

Shakshuka with Chive Flatbread

Robin

This classic North African and Middle Eastern dish has as many twists on its preparation as there are cooks who prepare it; this version is mine. I usually prefer to cook with fresh ingredients, so my pantry has few canned items. However, I always have canned crushed tomatoes, canned olives, and pepper paste on hand for convenience. Made with canned and fresh tomatoes, eggs, and smoky spices for a kick of heat, this shakshuka feels rustic as well as decadent. It's something that would feel as natural being prepared in a fancy kitchen as over an open fire. Serve it for breakfast, lunch, or dinner with unleavened chive bread alongside for dipping into that perfectly runny egg yolk. **Serves 6**

Flatbread

2 cups all-purpose flour, plus more for dusting

1 cup cold water

1 bunch chives, finely chopped

½ teaspoon salt

2 tablespoons olive oil

1 teaspoon coarse salt

Shakshuka

2 tablespoons olive oil

1 medium red onion, finely chopped

2 garlic cloves, minced

2 large bell peppers, preferably 1 orange/yellow and 1 green, seeded and very thinly sliced

1 (15-ounce) can crushed tomatoes

2 teaspoons harissa paste

1 tablespoon smoked paprika

½ teaspoon salt

3 medium plum tomatoes, thinly sliced

6 eggs

1 bunch flat-leaf parsley, roughly chopped

6 black olives, pitted and thinly sliced

6 green olives stuffed with pimentos

⅓ cup crumbled feta cheese

---

1. Preheat the oven to 400 degrees F.

2. In a large bowl, combine the flour, water, chives, and salt. Knead for a few minutes, adding flour as needed, until the dough comes together into a ball and is no longer sticky.

3. Cut the dough into six balls. Working with one at a time, flatten and roll them out into 4-inch-long oblongs about ¼ inch thick. Brush the dough with some of the olive oil.

4. Heat a large skillet or griddle over high heat until it's piping hot. Working in batches as necessary, place the dough, oiled side down, in the hot pan and cook until dark golden color on the bottom, about 2 minutes. Brush the top with a little more olive oil and flip it over. Cook, watching closely so it doesn't burn, until the other side gets a nice color, 1–2 minutes. Transfer the flatbread to a wire rack and sprinkle with coarse salt.

5. Heat the olive oil in a large cast iron skillet over medium heat (to cut down on dishes, you can use the same skillet you used to make the flatbread). Add the red onion and cook until it begins to

caramelize and get nice brown bits on the edges. Add the garlic, bell peppers, crushed tomatoes, harissa paste, paprika, and salt and cook, stirring, until the sauce starts to bubble and thicken, about 5 minutes; take care not to overcook the peppers. Turn off the heat.

6. Lay a few sliced tomatoes on top of the shakshuka. Make six indentations in the sauce and carefully crack one egg into each indentation. Immediately put the skillet in the oven and bake for about 7 minutes, until the eggs are cooked but still jiggle a bit.

7. Remove from the oven and sprinkle with the chopped parsley, olives, and feta. Scoop some of the shakshuka (including 1 egg) into each serving dish and place 1 flatbread on the edge.

Tortilla Española
Spanish Potato Omelet

Alejandra

A mainstay at tapas bars throughout Spain, tortilla española (or tortilla de patatas, as it's known locally) is a simple potato and onion omelet that can be enjoyed at any time of the day. When I was growing up, the Spanish omelet was my mom's go-to dish for weekend family brunches and post-church meals. As I grew older, I took over making it, and it's since become one of my own never-fail dishes to serve when entertaining. The tortilla can be served hot in thick wedges, or cut into smaller cubes and served chilled or at room temperature as a party appetizer with dollops of aioli. But my favorite way to enjoy tortilla española is the way I learned from my Tio Alonso, who is originally from Madrid. He taught me to make a bocadillo (a Spanish sandwich) with a thick slice of omelet tucked into a generously buttered crusty baguette. Feel free to add sliced cured Spanish chorizo, jamón serrano, or roasted red peppers to your tortilla mixture before cooking. **Serves 6**

2 cups extra-virgin olive oil

3 large Yukon Gold potatoes (about 1½ pounds), peeled and cut into ¼-inch-thick slices

1 large yellow onion, thinly sliced

1 teaspoon kosher salt, divided, plus more to taste

8 large eggs

1. Heat the olive oil in a 10-inch nonstick skillet over medium heat. Add the sliced potatoes and onion and allow to simmer gently in the oil, stirring occasionally, until the potatoes are fork-tender, 15–20 minutes. Keep an eye on the potatoes and adjust the temperature if it gets too hot. The potatoes should simmer, not fry.

2. Place a mesh strainer or colander over a bowl and drain the potatoes and onion. Reserve the oil. Transfer the potatoes and onion to a bowl and season with ½ teaspoon of the salt. Toss to combine, taste, and add more salt as needed.

3. In a separate large bowl, combine the 8 eggs and remaining ½ teaspoon salt and beat vigorously until light and frothy. Add the eggs to the potato and onion mixture and fold gently until combined.

4. Wipe the nonstick skillet clean, then add about ¼ cup of the reserved oil. Heat over medium heat until the oil is hot and shimmering, then add the egg and potato mixture, using a silicone spatula to spread the mixture out evenly. As the eggs cook, use the spatula to pull the mixture in from the sides toward the center, working your way around the pan and repeating until the edges are fully cooked and the center top is barely set, about 5 minutes.

5. Working over the sink or a counter (not the stove), invert a 10-inch plate over the skillet. Place your hand firmly on the bottom of the plate and quickly flip the plate and skillet over to turn the omelet out onto the plate. Add an additional 2 tablespoons of the reserved oil to the pan, then slide the omelet, with the wet side down, back into the skillet. Continue to cook, once again pulling in at the sides with the spatula, until fully set, about 3 minutes.

6. Slide or flip the tortilla out onto a clean platter and let stand for 5 minutes before serving.

Potato Crust Herb Quiche

Robin

The picky eaters in my family light up when they see this garden-fresh quiche. The crust, based on a traditional Jewish potato latke, gets a Mediterranean twist with a cheesy herb and tomato filling. This dish is gluten-free and meat-free, which can satisfy everyone who sits down at your table. **Makes 1 quiche; serves 8–10**

Potato crust

3 (8-ounce) russet potatoes, peeled and cut into large chunks

1 (8-ounce) onion, peeled and cut into large chunks

1 tablespoon potato starch or cornstarch

1½ teaspoons fine sea salt or 1 tablespoon kosher salt

Pinch cayenne pepper

1 tablespoon olive oil

1 tablespoon unsalted butter

Quiche

1 tablespoon olive oil

Juice of ½ lemon

2 garlic cloves, minced

1½ cups chopped spinach

8 large eggs

1½ cups shredded cheese, such as Mexican blend

Salt to taste

Cayenne pepper to taste

2 tablespoons fresh oregano leaves

2–3 plum tomatoes, thinly sliced

Avocado

2 ripe avocados, peeled and pitted

1 garlic clove, minced

Juice of 1 lime

1 small bunch flat-leaf parsley, chopped

1 tablespoon olive oil

Salt and ground black pepper to taste

1. Preheat the oven to 425 degrees F.

2. To make the potato crust, in a food processor fitted with the grating attachment, grate the potatoes and onion. Place a handful of the grated mixture onto a clean, lint-free towel, twist it shut, and wring it out tightly over the sink to release as much liquid as possible. Transfer the wrung-out grated mixture to a bowl. Keep squeezing the excess water out of the rest of the grated mixture until all of the mixture is in the bowl.

3. Sprinkle in the potato starch, salt, and cayenne and mix well. Drizzle in the olive oil and mix again.

4. Put the butter in a 10-inch deep-dish pie pan and place it in the oven just long enough to melt. Remove the pan from the oven and brush the melted butter across the bottom and up the sides of the pan.

5. Transfer the potato mixture to the buttered pan. Press the mixture onto the bottom and up the sides, forming a crust no more than ½ inch thick. Depending on the size of the potatoes, you may have excess grated potato-onion mixture. Bake for 40–50 minutes, or until the crust is golden brown.

(recipe continues)

6. While the crust is baking, mix the quiche filling. Drizzle the olive oil into a skillet and add the lemon juice and garlic. Cook over medium heat, stirring so the garlic doesn't burn.

7. Add the spinach to the pan, cover, and wait for the spinach to begin to wilt. Remove the lid, stir quickly, and leave it on the heat only long enough to wilt. Remove the pan from the heat and set aside to cool.

8. In a large bowl with a hand mixer, whisk the eggs until light and fluffy. Stir in the cheese and season with salt and cayenne. Fold in the spinach and then the oregano.

9. Remove the potato crust from the oven and lower the oven temperature to 375 degrees F. Place a long strip of foil around the top edges of the crust so it won't burn.

10. Pour the egg mixture into the potato crust. Arrange the tomatoes slices decoratively on top of the egg mixture. Place the quiche on a rimmed baking sheet and bake for 30–35 minutes, or until the egg mixture is set in the center and no longer jiggles.

11. While the quiche bakes, in a bowl, mash the avocados with the garlic, lime juice, parsley, and olive oil. Season with salt and pepper. Mix to the desired chunkiness.

12. Let the quiche cool, then cut into 8–10 slices. Place a slice of quiche on each plate with a dollop of the avocado mixture on top and serve.

Maple Pumpkin Bread

Robin

Nothing says fall to me like pumpkin, maple, and autumn spice flavors in a quick bread! Autumn in Maryland always renews my desire to get back into the kitchen and warm the house with baked goods after a long, hot summer. Living in an area with lots of nearby pumpkin patches, I was inspired to create this maple pumpkin bread. I gift this delicious loaf to family and friends with a recipe card attached. **Makes 5 mini loaves (3 x 5-inch pans), or 1 large loaf (5 x 9-inch pan) plus 2–3 bonus muffins; serves 10**

12 tablespoons (1½ sticks) unsalted butter, melted and cooled

1 cup white sugar

1 cup maple syrup

2 large eggs

1 (15-ounce can) pumpkin puree

2 cups all-purpose flour

1½ teaspoons baking powder

½ teaspoon baking soda

½ teaspoon fine sea salt

1½ tablespoons ground cinnamon

1 teaspoon ground ginger

½ teaspoon ground nutmeg

½ teaspoon ground cloves

½ teaspoon ground allspice

Maple drizzle

2 tablespoons unsalted butter

¼ cup maple syrup

¾ cup powdered sugar

Maple leaf hard candy, for garnish (optional)

Chocolate drizzle

2 ounces dark or milk chocolate

¼ teaspoon allspice

¼ teaspoon cinnamon

1. Preheat the oven to 350 degrees F. Spray 5 mini loaf pans (3 x 5 inches) or 1 large loaf pan (5 x 9 inches) with nonstick cooking spray, and have a muffin tin ready for excess batter.

2. In the bowl of a stand mixer fitted with the paddle attachment, beat the melted butter, sugar, and maple syrup together until light and fluffy.

3. In a small bowl, whisk together the eggs and pumpkin puree. Add the pumpkin mixture to the butter mixture, beating until incorporated. The mixture will look slightly broken at this point.

4. In a separate small bowl, sift together the flour, baking powder, baking soda, salt, and spices. Add the dry ingredients to the batter and blend until just incorporated. The batter will be thick.

5. If making mini loaves, divide the batter evenly among the 5 prepared pans and level the tops with an offset spatula. If making one large loaf, fill the prepared pan so that the batter comes up to ½ inch from the top when leveled off. If you have extra batter left over, you might have enough to make 2 or 3 bonus muffins; spray the cups of the muffin tin before filling.

(recipe continues)

6. Bake until the center springs back when pressed with a finger, about 45 minutes for mini loaves or 55–60 minutes for one large loaf. (Bonus muffins will bake in about 25 minutes.) Transfer to a wire rack to cool.

7. To make the maple drizzle, melt the butter in a small saucepan over low heat until it foams and then the foam dies back and the butter becomes a light caramel color. Remove from the heat and whisk in the maple syrup and powdered sugar to make a slightly thick but pourable glaze. You can adjust the consistency as desired: for a thin, translucent glaze, use less sugar; for an almost frosting-like glaze, add more sugar.

8. To make the chocolate drizzle, in a microwave or double boiler, melt the chocolate with the spices.

9. Remove the bread from the pan(s). Drizzle the glaze(s) over the top and place a maple leaf candy on top for garnish, if you like.

Desserts and Pastry

Tres Leches Cake 207

Mexican Mantecadas
with Lime Atole 209

Tahini Custard Pie 212

Almond and Oat Fig Tart 215

Button Cup Tarts
with Homemade Almond Milk 218

Baklawa 221

Tita Mirla's Famous Turon 224
(Banana Fritters)

Torrejas 225
(Spanish-Style French Toast with Anise Syrup)

Cranberry and White Chocolate Oatmeal
Cookies with Sour Cream Frosting
with Iced Chai 227

Italian Christmas Cookies: Biscotti,
Butterballs, and Pignoli 229

Cannoli Dip 233

Alejandra's Arroz con Leche 237
(Rice Pudding with Rum-Soaked Cherries)

Grilled Mango Sticky Rice 238

Tres Leches Cake

Silvia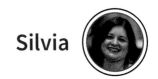

Rich, sweet, and delicious, this cake has evolved over time as I have adjusted the traditional recipe's ingredients and made a few additions of my own, like California strawberries, blueberries, edible flowers, and homemade whipped cream—all of which complement this classic yet contemporary dessert beautifully. Served well chilled, tres leches cake (or "three milks cake") resides in the pantheon of great Mexican show-stoppers. The secret is the balance between the dry and wet parts: too wet and you lose the structure and the bite of the crumb; too dry and you lose the creamy mouthfeel that makes it famous. **Makes 1 cake; serves 16**

Unsalted butter, for greasing

2 cups all-purpose flour

1 tablespoon baking powder

6 large eggs, at room temperature

2 cups white sugar

2 teaspoons vanilla extract

½ cup whole milk

1 (14-ounce) can sweetened condensed milk

1 (12-ounce) can evaporated milk

1 cup half-and-half

3 cups heavy cream

¾ cup powdered sugar

1 tablespoon vanilla extract

2 pounds fresh strawberries, divided (1 pound hulled and finely chopped, and 1 pound whole for garnish)

1 pint fresh blueberries, for garnish

Fresh mint leaves, for garnish (optional)

16 edible flowers, for garnish (optional)

1. Preheat the oven to 350 degrees F. Grease two 9 x 13-inch baking pans with butter, then line the bottoms and sides with parchment paper.

2. Sift the flour and baking powder together and set aside.

3. In a mixer with the paddle attachment, beat the eggs and white sugar until light and fluffy, 8–10 minutes. Add the vanilla and milk and mix to blend.

4. Using a silicone spatula, fold the dry ingredients into the batter until combined and no lumps remain. Be careful not to overmix.

5. Pour the batter into the prepared pans, dividing evenly, and bake for 12–15 minutes, or until a toothpick inserted into the middle comes out clean. The tops should be a deep golden brown. Remove the cakes from the oven and let them cool for 5 minutes.

6. Meanwhile, combine the sweetened condensed milk, evaporated milk, and half-and-half using a countertop blender or immersion blender, pureeing until smooth and evenly mixed.

7. Pour half of the milk mixture over one of the warm cakes slowly until it is absorbed. Repeat with the second cake and the remaining milk mixture. Let the cakes cool completely, then cover and place them in the fridge for at least 3 hours or overnight.

(recipe continues)

8. To make the whipped cream, in a mixer with the whisk attachment, whip the cream until thickened but not fully whipped, 2–3 minutes. Add the powdered sugar and vanilla and continue to whip until the cream forms soft peaks. Cover and place in the refrigerator for at least 3 hours.

9. When ready to assemble, flip one sponge cake out onto a serving dish and remove the parchment paper from the bottom and sides. Spread half of the whipped cream evenly over the top of the cake and sprinkle with the chopped strawberries. Carefully flip the second sponge cake on top of the first cake and remove the parchment paper. Use the remainder of the whipped cream to frost the top of the cake and garnish with the whole strawberries, as well as the blueberries, mint leaves, and edible flowers, if using. Cut into 16 pieces and serve.

Mexican Mantecadas

with Lime Atole

Silvia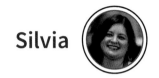

One type of Mexican pan dulce, mantecadas look like cupcakes, but their texture and crusty tops make them more muffin-like. Topping them with whipped cream takes them to a whole new level. A very traditional, corn-based Mexican hot beverage that can be made in a multitude of flavors, lime atole's citrus notes perfectly complement the mantecadas. **Makes about 15 mantecadas**

---

3 large eggs

¾ cup white sugar

2 teaspoons vanilla extract

½ cup whole milk

Grated zest of 1 orange

¾ cup vegetable oil

1⅔ cups all-purpose flour

2 teaspoons baking powder

½ teaspoon salt

Orange slices, for garnish (optional)

Whipped cream

1 cup heavy cream

¼ cup powdered sugar

1 teaspoon vanilla extract

---

1. Preheat the oven to 350 degrees F. Line two muffin tins with paper liners (15 cups total).

2. In a stand mixer with the whisk attachment, whip the eggs and white sugar until light and fluffy, about 10 minutes. Add the vanilla, milk, and orange zest and slowly whisk to combine. Pour in the oil slowly while the machine is running at low speed.

3. In a small bowl, sift together the flour, baking powder, and salt. Using a silicone spatula, fold the dry ingredients into the wet mixture until well incorporated, removing as many lumps as possible without overmixing.

4. Divide the mixture into the lined muffin tins, filling each cup three-quarters of the way. Bake for 18–20 minutes, or until golden brown. Transfer to a wire rack and let cool.

5. To make the whipped cream, in a stand mixer with the whisk attachment, whip together the cream, powdered sugar, and vanilla until soft peaks form, 2–3 minutes.

6. Top each mantecada with a dollop of whipped cream and a small piece of orange and serve with a glass of atole (recipe follows).

Lime Atole

5 cups whole milk

Zest of 2 large limes, peeled off in strips

¾ cup white sugar

1 cup water

¼ cup cornstarch

1. Combine the milk, lime peel, and sugar in a medium saucepan. Place the pan over high heat and stir until the sugar is dissolved.

2. Meanwhile, in a small bowl, whisk together the water and cornstarch until the cornstarch is completely dissolved.

3. When the milk starts to simmer, add the cornstarch mixture, whisking constantly. Lower the heat to medium-high and cook, stirring continuously, for 5 minutes, or until slightly thickened. Strain and serve.

Tahini Custard Pie

Robin

This pie was created in tribute to my mother, the best pie baker I have ever known, who took all her pie recipes with her when she passed. I'm honored to share this recipe, inspired by memories from my Syrian heritage. Like in the story of "Ali Baba and the Forty Thieves," "sesame" is the magic word in this recipe—offered up in the form of this tahini and cardamom custard in a toasted sesame pie crust. I think my mom would approve! **Makes 1 pie; serves 8–10**

Pie crust

1½ cups all-purpose flour, plus more for dusting

½ cup sesame flour (see note)

⅓ cup white sugar

½ teaspoon fine sea salt

8 tablespoons (1 stick) cold unsalted butter

¼ cup cold whole milk

1 large egg white (save the yolk for the custard)

2 tablespoons heavy cream

¼ cup white sesame seeds

Custard

1 cup heavy cream

2 large eggs, plus 2 large egg yolks

¾ cup white sugar

⅓ cup farina, such as Cream of Wheat

¼ cup tahini

1 teaspoon vanilla extract

1 teaspoon ground cinnamon

½ teaspoon ground cardamom

½ teaspoon fine sea salt

1 tablespoon turbinado sugar

Whipped cream

1 cup heavy cream

¼ cup powdered sugar

2 tablespoons ground cinnamon

Toasted white sesame seeds, for garnish

---

1. To make the crust, in a food processor, combine both flours, the sugar, salt, and butter and pulse until it crumbles together.

2. In a small bowl, whisk together the milk and egg white.

3. With the machine running, pour the milk mixture into the flour mixture until it comes together. Gather the dough into a ball and wrap with plastic wrap. Place the dough in the refrigerator and let it chill for at least 3 hours for easier rolling.

4. About 30 minutes before you are ready to form the crust, remove the dough from the fridge. Grease a 10-inch deep-dish pie pan.

5. On a floured surface, roll out the dough to ¼ inch thick and place it in the prepared pie pan. There may be a little bit of excess dough. Crimp the edges decoratively. Place the crust in the freezer for about 30 minutes to help hold its shape when baking. Meanwhile, make the custard base.

6. In an electric mixer with the whisk attachment, whip the cream to soft peaks. Transfer the whipped cream to a smaller bowl and wipe out the mixer bowl.

(recipe continues)

7. In the cleaned bowl, whip the whole eggs, egg yolks, and sugar with the whisk attachment until light and fluffy. Gently whisk in the farina, tahini, vanilla, cinnamon, cardamom, and salt, until just incorporated. Fold in the whipped cream, mixing until just combined.

8. Preheat the oven to 375 degrees F.

9. Remove the crust from the freezer and brush the edges of the crust with the cream. While holding the crust over parchment paper, sprinkle the sesame seeds along the edges, tipping the crust on its side as needed to help the seeds adhere. Shake out the excess seeds that have fallen into the base of the crust.

10. Gently pour the custard base into the pie crust, taking care not to disturb the seeds. Sprinkle the turbinado sugar all over the top of the custard.

11. Bake for 10 minutes, then lower the oven temperature to 350 degrees F and bake for another 25–30 minutes, until the center is domed and springy and the whole pie shakes as one unit when tapped lightly. Set aside to cool completely.

12. To make the whipped cream, in an electric mixer with the whisk attachment, whip the cream with the powdered sugar and cinnamon. Cover and chill until ready to serve.

13. Once the pie has cooled completely, using a sharp long knife, cut the pie into 8–10 slices. Serve each slice with a dollop of whipped cream and a sprinkle of toasted white sesame seeds.

Note: You can substitute oat flour for the sesame flour, but it will change the flavor.

Almond and Oat Fig Tart

Robin

The fig begins its life not as a fruit but rather as an inverted flower. This reminds me that our beauty must flower first on the inside. This beautiful tart, filled with custard and topped with fruit, is wonderful to make in summer and early fall when fresh figs are in season; I like Mission figs for their striking color.
Makes 1 tart; serves 8–10

Crust

2 cups old-fashioned rolled oats

1 cup crushed almonds or almond flour

4 tablespoons (½ stick) unsalted butter, at room temperature

2 tablespoons white sugar

1 tablespoon grated orange zest

½ teaspoon ground cardamom

¼ teaspoon fine sea salt

3 large egg whites

Custard

1½ cups mascarpone cheese

1 large egg, plus 3 large egg yolks

½ cup white sugar

½ teaspoon orange blossom water

Grated zest of 1 orange

¾ cup heavy cream

10–12 Mission figs, pitted and sliced ⅛ to ¼ inch thick

2 tablespoons turbinado sugar

Whipped cream

1 cup heavy cream

2 tablespoons powdered sugar

¼ teaspoon orange blossom water

¼ teaspoon ground cardamom

Fig glaze

1 cup fig jam

2 tablespoons white sugar

¼ cup almond liqueur

2 tablespoons fig balsamic vinegar

Assembly

8–10 Johnny-jump-ups or other purple and yellow edible flowers (optional)

1. To make the crust, grind the oats and almonds in a food processor until broken down but still a little flaky. Add the butter, white sugar, orange zest, cardamom, and salt. Pulse several times until the butter is evenly incorporated into the oat mixture. Add the egg whites and pulse until a slightly wet and crumbly dough is formed.

2. Press the dough ¼ inch thick into the bottom and up the sides of a 10-inch nonstick tart pan with a removable bottom. There may be a little bit of excess dough. Set the tart on a rimmed baking sheet and place in the freezer until ready to bake.

3. To make the custard, preheat the oven to 350 degrees F.

(recipe continues)

4. In a bowl, whisk together the mascarpone, whole egg and egg yolks, white sugar, orange blossom water, and orange zest until smooth. Add the cream and whisk until fully incorporated. Pour the batter into the frozen tart crust. Bake the tart for 30–35 minutes, or until it is partially set.

5. Carefully remove the tart from the oven and decoratively place the fig slices on top. Sprinkle the entire top with the turbinado sugar. Return the tart to the oven, being careful not to disturb the filling, and bake for another 15–20 minutes, until the filling is set and firm. Remove from the oven and let cool completely.

6. To make the topping, whip the cream, powdered sugar, orange blossom water, and cardamom together until soft peaks form. Set aside.

7. To make the fig glaze, in a small saucepan, bring the fig jam, white sugar, liqueur, and vinegar to a boil and allow to thicken, about 5 minutes. Set aside.

8. To assemble, remove the cooled tart from the pan by pressing up on the bottom and removing the rim. Cut into 8–10 slices. Place a slice of tart on each plate. Spoon a dollop of whipped cream on top of the tart. Drizzle on a little bit of fig glaze. If desired, garnish with a flower on top.

Button Cup Tarts
with Homemade Almond Milk

Robin

Inspired by the mouse who was a tailor in the Beatrix Potter book *The Tailor of Gloucester*, I made these treats for the first time for my daughter Leah's third birthday. Cookies made to look like buttons sit on top of tart shells filled with yummy jam and almond butter. Leah, being the youngest and only girl, was doted on by her big brother Tomio, the oldest. The kids would eat these tarts for Leah's birthday and the occasional tea party she might have hosted as a little girl. Tomio would often help me make them, and we would share joy in preparing something special for Leah. **Makes about 16 mini tarts**

Strawberry jam

2 cups chopped strawberries

1 cup sugar

3 tablespoons white balsamic vinegar

2 tablespoons lemon juice

1 rosemary sprig

1 teaspoon cornstarch

1 teaspoon water

Pastry

1 cup (2 sticks) unsalted butter, at room temperature

8 ounces cream cheese, at room temperature

¾ cup sugar

3 cups all-purpose flour, plus more for rolling

¼ teaspoon fine sea salt

1 large egg

1 tablespoon water

Almond butter

2 cups raw whole almonds with skins

2 tablespoons honey

½ teaspoon ground ginger

½ teaspoon salt

½ cup plain unsweetened whole-milk Greek yogurt

1. To make the strawberry jam, combine the strawberries, sugar, vinegar, and lemon juice in a food processor and puree. Transfer to a saucepan, add the rosemary sprig, and bring to a boil, then lower the heat and simmer for 15 minutes. Remove and discard the rosemary sprig.

2. In a small bowl, whisk together cornstarch and water. Slowly add the cornstarch mixture to the strawberry mixture, whisking constantly. Whisk the jam and continue to cook until thickened. Remove the pan from the heat and transfer the jam to a larger bowl. Place the bowl in the refrigerator to cool faster.

3. To make the pastry, preheat the oven to 350 degrees F.

4. In a food processor, combine the butter, cream cheese, sugar, flour, and salt and process until it comes together in a ball.

5. Turn out the dough onto a work surface and roll it out to about ¼ inch thick. Using a round cookie cutter the diameter of the exterior of the mini tart molds, cut 16 circles. Press the dough into the tart molds, pressing the dough down into the bottom and up the sides. Trim the top edge with a knife or by pinching the dough with your thumb to create a flat edge along the top of the tart mold.

6. Place the tart molds in the freezer to help them hold their shape.

7. Line a rimmed baking sheet with parchment paper. Using a round cookie cutter the diameter of the interior of the mini tart mold, cut 16 circles for the "button" tops. Place the "buttons" on the lined baking sheet. To make "button holes" in the tops, use the narrow end of a chopstick or a skewer to make four little holes in a square pattern.

8. In a small bowl, whisk together the egg and water for the egg wash. Brush only the button tops with the egg wash.

(recipe continues)

9. Bake the button tops for 15 minutes, or until golden. Set aside to cool on a wire rack. If the button holes need redefining, do so while the tops are still warm.

10. Remove the tart molds from the freezer. Line each one with a paper cupcake liner and fill with pie weights or dried beans/rice. Bake for about 20 minutes, or until the edges are starting to turn brown. Remove the paper liners and pie weights and continue to bake the tarts for another 8 minutes, or until golden. Remove from the oven and let cool slightly. While the tarts are still a little warm, remove the tart shells from the molds (they have a tendency to stick if removed when completely cooled).

11. To make the almond butter, put the almonds in a small skillet, cover, and cook for about 5 minutes. Take care not to let them burn. Remove from the heat and cool for a few minutes, then transfer the almonds to a food processor. Add the honey, ginger, and salt and puree, scraping down the sides as needed, until the mixture turns into a paste. This can take about 10 minutes. Add the yogurt at the end and puree to a creamy butter. Transfer to a small bowl.

12. To assemble the tarts, place a small spoonful of almond butter in each pastry shell, then add a small dollop of strawberry jam. Put the button top on and press gently. Serve on a small plate with almond milk in a shot glass.

Homemade Almond Milk

3 cups water

1 cup blanched almonds

1 teaspoon white sugar

1. In a large pot, bring the water to a boil.

2. Meanwhile, grind the blanched almonds and sugar in a food processor until a fine crumb is achieved.

3. Carefully add the nut mixture to the boiling water. Cover and simmer over low heat for 20 minutes. Let cool.

4. Press the mixture through a fine-mesh sieve or nut bag, squeezing all the liquid from the almonds. Chill the milk until ready to serve. Shake before serving.

Baklawa

Robin

Traditionally, at Middle Eastern gatherings, a dessert spread of many selections greets the guests first. It is always an indication of how grand the meal being served will be. This dish is near to my heart as my mother used to prepare it for parties when I was a kid. This recipe makes two flavors of pastries: one flavored with rosewater honey and nuts and the other with arak or ouzo (anise-flavored spirits), honey, dates, and nuts. The garnish, Jordan almonds, are traditional at any important celebration. While it has never been traditional to use an egg in baklawa, it has become my healthy approach and technique for holding together the nut fillings—it lets you cut back on the sugar traditionally used to hold them together so they don't fall out at first bite. **Serves 24 (makes about 24 pieces of each flavor)**

---

1 pound frozen phyllo dough, thawed

Nut filling

1 cup (2 sticks) unsalted butter

12 ounces walnuts

12 ounces shelled pistachios

1 tablespoon sugar

1 tablespoon ground cinnamon

1 teaspoon ground mace

½ teaspoon ground cloves

Salt to taste

1 large egg

Date filling

1 pound pitted dates

1 cup blanched, slivered almonds

1 tablespoon arak or ouzo

2 tablespoons cocoa powder

1 teaspoon ground cardamom

Salt to taste

Honey drizzle and garnish

⅔ cup honey, divided

½ teaspoon rosewater

1 tablespoon arak or ouzo

3 red, bright pink, or white food-safe roses

1 cup Jordan almonds (multicolored pastel)

---

1. Preheat the oven to 350 degrees F. Line two rimmed baking sheets with parchment paper.

2. To prepare the nut filling, melt the butter in a small saucepan over low heat. Keep warm.

3. In a food processor, combine the walnuts, pistachios, sugar, cinnamon, mace, cloves, and salt and process until finely ground. Add the egg and blend until it is clumpy and wet.

4. Unroll the phyllo on a flat surface. Cover with a towel or plastic wrap so it doesn't dry out.

5. Place one sheet of phyllo on a parchment-covered work surface with one long side of the rectangle closest to you. Brush with some of the melted butter. Place a second sheet of phyllo on top of the buttered sheet and brush the second sheet with butter. Repeat this process until you have five layers of buttered phyllo sheets. Make sure to keep the extra phyllo covered between each step.

6. Divide the nut filling in half. Lay one half of the filling in the shape of a log at the edge of the phyllo closest to you, along one long side of the rectangle. Gently lift the phyllo up and over the nut filling, then continue rolling it away from you to form a tight roll.

(recipe continues)

7. Transfer the log to one of the lined baking sheets, leaving space for a second log. Using a serrated knife, cut halfway through the log with 10–12 slices on the bias 1–2 inches apart (like a baguette). Brush the top with melted butter.

8. Repeat the whole process again with five more sheets of phyllo, the remainder of the nut filling, and more melted butter.

9. To prepare the date filling, in a food processor, combine the dates, almonds, arak, cocoa powder, cardamom, and salt. Process until ground finely. It will form a clumpy ball.

10. Place one sheet of phyllo on a parchment-covered work surface with one long side of the rectangle closest to you. Brush with some of the melted butter. Place a second sheet of phyllo on top of the buttered sheet and brush the second sheet with butter. Repeat this process until you have five layers of buttered phyllo sheets. Make sure to keep the extra phyllo covered between each step.

11. Divide the date filling in half. Lay one half of the filling in the shape of a log at the edge of the phyllo closest to you, along one long side of the rectangle. Gently lift the phyllo up and over the date filling, then continue rolling it away from you to form a tight roll.

12. Transfer the log to the second lined baking sheet, leaving space for a second log. Using a serrated knife, cut halfway through the log with 10–12 slices on the bias 1–2 inches apart (like a baguette). Brush the top with melted butter.

13. Repeat the whole process again with five more sheets of phyllo, the remainder of the date filling, and more melted butter.

14. Bake the nut and date pastries for 30–35 minutes, or until golden brown.

15. While the pastries are baking, make the honey drizzle. For the nut pastry, in a small bowl, whisk together ⅓ cup of the honey and the rosewater. For the date pastry, in a small bowl, whisk together the remaining ⅓ cup honey and the arak.

16. Stack about 10 rose petals together, then tightly roll the stack like a cigar. Cut the roll crosswise into chiffonade (thin ribbons). Set aside.

17. When the baklawa is finished baking, remove from them from the oven and let cool for 10–15 minutes. Using a serrated knife, cut each slit all the way through. If the logs are still too hot, they will crumble apart, and if they cool too much, the phyllo shatters and falls off.

18. Gently drizzle the honey-rosewater mixture over the nut pastry slices. Sprinkle on the sliced rose petals to stick to the honey. Allow to sit for 10 minutes to soak up the honey.

19. Gently drizzle the honey-arak mixture over the top of the date pastry slices. Allow to sit for 10 minutes to soak up the honey.

20. Place the pastries on serving dishes. Garnish with additional whole rose petals and Jordan almonds.

Tita Mirla's Famous Turon

Banana Fritters

Leah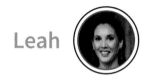

My aunt Tita Mirla is known for her sweets. One of my first introductions to the Filipino dessert known as turon was at a very young age, and I have Tita Mirla to thank. My family would always host Thanksgiving, and my mom's side of the family would bring Filipino dishes to make our Thanksgiving meals multicultural. To me there is nothing better than fried banana served à la mode, which is why I loved eating this as a child and have introduced it to my kids. The jackfruit is a nice addition of flavor, although it's not necessary. I use canned jackfruit instead of fresh because it is always readily available. I love this dish so much—it brings back so many childhood memories—that I include a version of it on the dessert menu at one of my restaurants. **Makes 16 fritters**

¾ cup light brown sugar

1½ teaspoons ground cinnamon

1 large egg

1 tablespoon cold water

16 spring roll wrappers

4 small ripe bananas, peeled, halved crosswise, and then halved lengthwise

4 pieces canned young jackfruit, cut into quarters

Vegetable oil, for deep frying

Vanilla ice cream, for serving (optional)

---

1. Mix together the brown sugar and cinnamon in a small dish. In another small dish, whisk together the egg and water.

2. Place a spring roll wrapper in front of you in a diamond shape. Lay 1 piece of banana and 1 piece of jackfruit (if using) two-thirds of the way down from the top and sprinkle with 1½ teaspoons of the sugar-cinnamon. Fold the sides in and then roll it up tightly from the bottom to the top to form a long cylinder. Brush the turon with egg wash to seal. Repeat with all wrappers and fruit.

3. Line a large plate or baking sheet with paper towels. In a high-sided sauté pan or wok, heat the oil over medium heat until it reaches 350 degrees F. Fry the turon in batches until golden brown, turning once. Drain on the paper towels. Serve with ice cream, if you like.

Torrejas

Spanish-Style French Toast
with Anise Syrup

Alejandra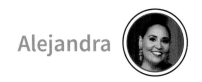

Torrejas is a Spanish dessert typically enjoyed just before Lent and then again during Easter in Spain and various parts of Latin America and the Caribbean. Similar to French toast, it's made with custard-soaked bread that's pan-fried. But unlike traditional French toast, torrejas are soaked completely through with a fragrant anise-scented honey and sugar syrup and served at room temperature. **Serves 6**

Anise syrup

1½ cups water

1 cup sugar

½ cup honey

1 tablespoon grated orange zest

½ teaspoon kosher salt

2 cinnamon sticks

½ teaspoon almond extract

¼ teaspoon anise extract

French toast

2 large eggs

1½ cups whole milk

½ teaspoon ground cinnamon

1 slightly stale loaf Cuban or French bread, sliced diagonally into 1½-inch-thick slices

4–6 tablespoons olive oil

Flaky sea salt, for garnish

1. Combine the water, sugar, honey, orange zest, salt, and cinnamon sticks in a medium saucepan and bring to a boil; boil for 1 minute. Lower the heat and simmer until reduced to a thin syrup, 7–10 minutes. Remove from the heat and stir in the extracts; set aside.

2. Whisk together the eggs, milk, and cinnamon in a shallow bowl. Dip the bread in the batter and let soak for 30 seconds to 1 minute (do not let the bread get too soggy).

3. Heat 2 tablespoons of the olive oil in a large skillet and fry the battered bread in batches until golden, about 3 minutes per side. Transfer to a slightly concave or rimmed serving platter. Repeat with the rest of the bread, adding more oil as needed.

4. Pour the syrup over the torrejas to cover them fully. Let soak for at least 30 minutes before serving, turning occasionally, or cover and chill overnight for better absorption. Top with a bit of flaky sea salt and serve chilled or at room temperature.

Cranberry and White Chocolate Oatmeal Cookies with Sour Cream Frosting

Brian

with Iced Chai

Oatmeal cookies have a special place in my heart. Throughout my mom's life, she'd always have some form of fresh baked cookie in her kitchen—usually oatmeal raisin. As time went on, she started adding white chocolate and replaced the raisins with dried cranberries. Instantly, they became my favorite. The evolution of those cookies into my version of oatmeal cream pies happened when I started playing tabletop role-playing games—I shared them with my friends and they became a game-day staple. This recipe is a fusion of both those memories. **Makes about 20 cookie sandwiches**

Cookies

1 cup (2 sticks) unsalted butter, at room temperature

1 cup light brown sugar

¼ cup white sugar

2 large eggs, at room temperature

1 tablespoon vanilla extract

1 tablespoon molasses

1½ cups all-purpose flour

1 teaspoon baking soda

1 teaspoon ground cardamom

½ teaspoon fine sea salt

3 cups old-fashioned rolled oats

1 cup dried cranberries

½ cup white chocolate chips

Sour cream frosting

1 cup (2 sticks) unsalted butter, at room temperature

2½ cups powdered sugar

½ cup full-fat sour cream, at room temperature

1 tablespoon vanilla extract

½ teaspoon fine sea salt

---

1. To make the cookies, using a stand mixer with the paddle attachment, cream the butter and both sugars together on medium speed until light and fluffy, about 10 minutes. Add the eggs and beat until combined, about 1 minute, scraping down the sides and bottom of the bowl as needed. Add the vanilla and molasses and mix until combined.

2. In a medium bowl, whisk together the flour, baking soda, cardamom, and salt. Add the dry ingredients to the wet ingredients and mix on low until combined. Slowly incorporate the oats, dried cranberries, and white chocolate chips on low speed.

3. Let the dough rest and set up for at least 30 minutes.

(recipe continues)

4. Preheat the oven to 350 degrees F. Line two rimmed baking sheets with parchment paper.

5. Using about 2 tablespoons per cookie, roll the dough into balls and place them on the lined baking sheets, spaced at least 2 inches apart. Press the tops down slightly to form patties.

6. Bake for 8–10 minutes, or until the sides are lightly browned and the centers look done.

7. Let the cookies cool on the baking sheets for 5 minutes, then transfer to a wire rack to cool completely.

8. To make the frosting, using a stand mixer with the paddle attachment, cream the butter on high speed for 5 minutes. Add the powdered sugar and slowly beat until it is fully incorporated. Add the sour cream, vanilla, and salt and mix on low until just incorporated. Transfer the frosting to a piping bag with a floret tip and place in the refrigerator to set.

9. When the cookies are cool and the frosting is set, pipe a dollop of frosting onto the flat side of a cookie. Find a cookie of the same size and shape and make a sandwich. Repeat to make all the sandwich cookies.

10. Serve with a glass of chilled chai tea.

Iced Chai

5 whole green cardamom pods

1 teaspoon whole black peppercorns

1 star anise

3 cups water

1 tablespoon peeled and thinly sliced ginger

3 whole cloves

3 tablespoons loose black tea leaves

1 tablespoon dark brown sugar

1 cup heavy cream

Ice cubes

1. In a saucepan, toast the cardamom, black peppercorns, and star anise over low heat, stirring often. Once toasted, remove from the pan and set aside.

2. Pour the water into the same pan and bring it to a boil.

3. While the water is coming to a boil, using a mortar and pestle, crush the ginger, cloves, cardamom, black peppercorns, and star anise into small pieces. When the water comes to a boil, add the spices to the pan.

4. Let the water boil for 1 minute, then reduce the heat to low. Add the tea leaves, cover, and simmer for 5 minutes, then turn off the heat and let steep for another 5 minutes.

5. Bring the pot back to low heat and add the brown sugar and heavy cream, whisking until the sugar is dissolved.

6. Remove from the heat, strain the tea mixture, and pour over ice to serve.

Italian Christmas Cookies: Biscotti, Butterballs, and Pignoli

Dan

These are very special cookies. Traditionally, my family makes these cookies only for Christmas and maybe weddings. On Christmas, the Rinaldis put these Italian holiday cookies out on a plate for Santa when he comes down the chimney. My mother always made cookies like these with my aunt, and they passed the tradition down to me. Making all three varieties makes for a special holiday display. For an easy but impressive garnish, lay a fork and spoon in the center of the plate. Put a spoonful of cocoa powder into a fine-mesh strainer and dust the cocoa over the platter. Carefully pick up the silverware and arrange the cookies around the stenciled pattern.

Biscotti

Makes 50–60 cookies

½ cup plus 2 tablespoons brown sugar

¼ cup plus 2 tablespoons white sugar

2 large eggs, plus 1 large egg yolk

2 teaspoons almond extract

1 cup all-purpose flour, plus more for dusting

1 teaspoon baking powder

⅛ teaspoon fine sea salt

1½ cups raw whole almonds (with skins)

1 tablespoon water

1 pound high-quality dark chocolate, such as Jacques Torres 60% dark chocolate

1. Preheat the oven to 375 degrees F. Line a rimmed baking sheet with parchment paper.

2. Using a stand mixer fitted with the paddle attachment, beat together both sugars, the 2 whole eggs, and the almond extract until light and fluffy. Add the flour, baking powder, and salt and mix until well combined. Add the almonds and blend until mixed in. The dough will be loose.

3. Divide the dough in half. On a floured surface, quickly roll each half into a long log the length of the baking sheet. Place the dough logs on the lined baking sheet, leaving space between the two logs.

4. Whisk together the egg yolk and water and brush the tops of the logs with the egg wash.

5. Bake for 20–25 minutes, rotating the pan halfway through, or until the logs are a deep golden brown and the centers spring back to the touch.

6. Transfer the logs to a wire rack and cool for 10–15 minutes before cutting. Lower the oven temperature to 325 degrees F. Using a serrated knife, slice the logs on a bias to make biscotti.

(recipe continues)

(If the log cools completely before cutting, it becomes brittle and just crumbles; if it is still too warm, the almonds roll out and the log breaks apart in chunks.)

7. Lay the biscotti slices on their sides on the same lined baking sheet and return them to the oven. Bake for 15–20 minutes, or until they are dried out with just a little bit of a toasted color. Transfer to a wire rack to cool completely.

8. Once the cookies are cooled, melt the chocolate in a double boiler or in the microwave. Dip one end of each cookie in the chocolate and place on the lined baking sheet. Refrigerate or freeze to help set up the chocolate.

Butterballs

Makes about 24 cookies

8 tablespoons (1 stick) unsalted butter, at room temperature

1 tablespoon plus 1 cup powdered sugar

½ teaspoon pure vanilla extract

1 cup all-purpose flour

¼ cup walnut pieces

1. Preheat the oven to 400 degrees F. Line a rimmed baking sheet with parchment paper.

2. In an electric mixer with the paddle attachment, cream together the butter and 1 tablespoon of the powdered sugar until soft and fluffy. Add the vanilla, flour, and walnuts and mix until incorporated.

3. Using a tablespoon, scoop equal portions of the dough. Roll the dough portions into balls and place on the lined baking sheet with a little bit of space in between (they do not spread when baking).

4. Bake for 15–20 minutes, or until the bottoms are deep golden brown. Transfer to a wire rack and let cool completely.

5. Once cooled, put the remaining 1 cup powdered sugar in a large plastic bag, add the cookies, and gently shake until coated. Remove the cookies from the bag and shake off the excess powdered sugar.

(recipe continues)

Pignoli

Makes about 32 cookies

½ cup white sugar

½ cup powdered sugar

¼–½ cup all-purpose flour

⅛ teaspoon fine sea salt

8 ounces almond paste

2 large egg whites

1 cup pine nuts

---

1. Preheat the oven to 350 degrees F. Line a rimmed baking sheet with parchment paper.

2. In a small bowl, sift together the white sugar, powdered sugar, ¼ cup of the flour, and the sea salt. Set aside.

3. Break up the almond paste and place it in a food processor. Add the egg whites and process until smooth.

4. Add the dry ingredients and process until smooth. Test the consistency: when scooped and placed on a baking sheet, the dough should be soft and settle into a dome but should not be too runny. If needed, add more flour one tablespoon at a time until a soft, not too stiff dough is formed.

5. Dip a tablespoon in a cup of water, then scoop the dough into equal portions. Place the scoops of dough on the lined baking sheet. Sprinkle the top of each cookie with pine nuts.

6. Bake the cookies for about 10 minutes, or until golden brown. Let the cookies cool completely on the baking sheet.

7. When cool, carefully lift the parchment paper and flip it over onto the baking sheet so the cookies are facing down. Using a wet paper towel, dampen the parchment paper, touching the backs of each cookie. Then very carefully, starting at one corner, gently lift the paper away from the cookie.

Cannoli Dip

Tony

Whether I am going to the park for a picnic or getting together with friends, this deconstructed cannoli dessert dip is my go-to; friends and family have requested the dish from me many times, and I love sharing the recipe. The homemade cannoli "chips" are a play on the classic cannoli shells, and paired with a creamy and rich dip with whipped ricotta and mascarpone cheeses, they make for an easy and fun dessert. Dunk and dip in. **Serves 12**

Dip

1 pound mascarpone cheese

1 pound whole-milk ricotta cheese

2 cups powdered sugar, plus more for garnish

2 teaspoons ground cinnamon

1 teaspoon ground nutmeg

1 teaspoon fine sea salt

1 tablespoon vanilla extract

Grated zest of 1 orange

2 cups mini semisweet chocolate chips, plus more for garnish

Cocoa powder, for garnish

Cannoli chips

2 cups all-purpose flour, plus more for dusting

3 tablespoons white sugar

½ teaspoon ground cinnamon

½ teaspoon fine sea salt

2 tablespoons cold unsalted butter

½ cup dry white wine

1 large egg, plus 1 large egg yolk

Vegetable oil, for deep frying

1. To make the dip, in a stand mixer with the whisk attachment, whip the mascarpone and ricotta at medium speed until combined and smooth. Sift and add 1 cup of the powdered sugar to the cheese mixture and whip for 30 seconds. Sift and add the second cup of powdered sugar and whip until just incorporated. Add the cinnamon, nutmeg, salt, vanilla, orange zest, and chocolate chips and whip until nicely combined and fluffy.

2. Transfer the dip to a large bowl and garnish with additional chocolate chips and a dusting of powdered sugar and cocoa powder. Cover with plastic wrap and refrigerate until ready to serve.

3. To make the cannoli chips, in a large bowl, whisk together the flour, sugar, cinnamon, and salt. Cut the butter into the flour using a pastry cutter until the flour looks wet and crumbly. Add the wine, egg, and egg yolk and stir with a silicone spatula until a dough forms.

4. Knead the dough for a couple of minutes on a lightly floured surface, until no dry flour remains. Wrap the dough in plastic wrap and refrigerate for at least 1 hour or overnight.

5. When ready to fry the chips, pour the oil into a large, heavy-bottomed pot and heat to 375 degrees F.

6. On a floured work surface, roll out the dough to ⅛ inch thick. The dough may be sticky, so add more flour to the surface as necessary. Slide an offset spatula under the dough to make sure it is not sticking.

(recipe continues)

7. With a pizza slicer or a long knife, cut the dough into the desired shapes, such as triangle chips or strips.

8. Working in small batches, fry the dough pieces for 3–4 minutes, or until a deep golden brown, flipping them halfway through cooking.

9. Remove from the oil and place on a wire cooling rack or a baking sheet lined with paper towels to cool.

10. Serve the fresh cannoli chips alongside the chilled cannoli filling. If you're making the cannoli chips ahead of time, let them cool completely before storing them in an airtight container.

Alejandra's Arroz con Leche

Alejandra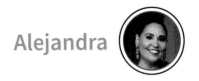

Rice Pudding with Rum-Soaked Cherries

Arroz con leche has long been one of my favorite desserts. This traditional Latin-style rice pudding is a bit looser in texture and flavored with cinnamon and fresh citrus zest.

When I was a kid, my dad would order rice pudding at a local diner, and the two of us would share it for dessert. Neither one of us was a fan of the raisins, so we'd leave them on the side. In this dessert, I decided to skip the raisins in favor of rum-soaked cherries, which add a slightly tropical and almost ambrosial flavor to the final dish.

This simple recipe can be served warm straight from the stove, or cold in small pudding cups. It's ideal for entertaining, but I confess that it's the leftovers that make me happiest, since I can enjoy them for breakfast while still in my pajamas, one spoonful at a time. **Serves 6–8**

---

1 cup dried cherries

1 cup dark rum

1 cup long-grain white rice

5 whole cloves

3 cinnamon sticks

1 vanilla bean, split lengthwise (optional)

1 tablespoon grated lemon zest

1 tablespoon grated orange zest

1 teaspoon kosher salt

4 cups water

1 large egg

2½ cups whole milk

1½ cups heavy cream

¾ cup sugar

1 tablespoon vanilla extract

Ground cinnamon, for garnish

---

1. Combine the cherries and rum in a small heatproof bowl and microwave for 1 minute. Set aside to soak while you prepare the pudding.

2. Combine the rice, cloves, cinnamon sticks, vanilla bean (if using), lemon zest, orange zest, salt, and water in a large, heavy-bottomed saucepan. Bring to a boil, then lower the heat and let simmer for 10 minutes, or until the water has mostly evaporated.

3. In a small bowl, whisk together the egg, milk, cream, sugar, and vanilla. Pour the mixture into the rice and stir until combined. Let the pudding simmer over medium-low heat, stirring occasionally, just until it starts to thicken, about 20 minutes. (The pudding will continue to thicken as it cools, so err on the side of stopping sooner for the silkiest texture.)

4. Remove from the heat. Remove and discard the cloves, cinnamon sticks, and vanilla bean (if used). Drain the cherries and stir them into the pudding. Serve warm or cold, with a sprinkle of cinnamon on top. Let the pudding cool before chilling.

Grilled Mango Sticky Rice

Foo

Instead of traditional desserts, my parents would hand all their kids fruit after a meal to satisfy our sweet tooth. This very lightly sweet dish reminds me of sitting at the dinner table with my family, whom I love so very much. Sticky rice is traditional to Vietnamese cuisine, and I added the mango for more sweetness and flavor. **Serves 10–12**

---

4 cups sweet rice

3 cups canned coconut milk, divided

3 cups water, divided

1 teaspoon sugar

1¼ teaspoons salt, divided

2 pandan leaves

2 tablespoons cornstarch

10 sweet orange mangoes, peeled, pitted, and sliced

2 tablespoons olive oil

3 tablespoons cayenne pepper

1 tablespoon coarse sea salt

¼ cup coarsely chopped roasted peanuts

---

1. Rinse the rice about five times, until the water is clear. Put the rice in a large pot and add 2 cups of the coconut milk, 2 cups of the water, the sugar, and 1 teaspoon of the salt.

2. Place the pandan leaves on top of the rice. Cover the pot and bring to a boil over high heat, about 10 minutes. Turn the heat down to low and cook until the rice absorbs all the liquid and is tender, about 8 minutes.

3. In a small pot, combine the remaining 1 cup coconut milk, remaining 1 cup water, remaining ¼ teaspoon salt, and cornstarch. Bring to a low boil and mix until the cornstarch is completely dissolved.

4. Coat the mangoes with the olive oil and sear on a grill pan to obtain grill marks.

5. Spoon some sticky rice into each bowl and top with the seared mangoes. Drizzle the coconut slurry over the rice and garnish with the cayenne pepper, coarse sea salt, and peanuts.

METRIC CONVERSIONS

US STANDARD	UNITED KINGDOM
¼ teaspoon	¼ teaspoon (scant)
½ teaspoon	½ teaspoon (scant)
¾ teaspoon	½ teaspoon (rounded)
1 teaspoon	¾ teaspoon (slightly rounded)
1 tablespoon	2½ teaspoons
¼ cup	¼ cup minus 1 dessert spoon
⅓ cup	¼ cup plus 1 teaspoon
½ cup	⅓ cup plus 2 dessert spoons
⅔ cup	½ cup plus 1 tablespoon
¾ cup	½ cup plus 2 tablespoons
1 cup	¾ cup plus 2 dessert spoons

INDEX

Salad